2018 Colouring Diary

I0480214

By Sassy Colouring

IF LOST PLEASE
RETURN TO:

My contact number is:

My email is:

My address is:

PERSONAL NOTES

Name: ____

Address: ____

____

Tel: ____

Email: ____

In case of emergency please contact:

Name: ____

Address: ____

____

Tel: ____

Email: ____

Personal Details:

Allergies: ____

Doctor: ____

Blood Type: ____

CONTACTS

Name:____
Address:______________________________________
____
Tel:____
Email:_______________________________________

Name:____
Address:______________________________________
____
Tel:____
Email:_______________________________________

Name:____
Address:______________________________________
____
Tel:____
Email:_______________________________________

Name:____
Address:______________________________________
____
Tel:____
Email:_______________________________________

Name:____
Address:______________________________________
____
Tel:____
Email:_______________________________________

DATES TO REMEMBER

YEAR IN PIXELS

	J	F	M	A	M	J	J	A	S	O	N	D
1												
2												
3												
4												
5												
6												
7												
8												
9												
10												
11												
12												
13												
14												
15												
16												
17												
18												
19												
20												
21												
22												
23												
24												
25												
26												
27												
28												
29												
30												
31												

Choose a colour to match you mood:

Colour	Mood	Colour	Mood
	Excited		Tired
	Happy		Sad
	Average		Angry

BOOKS TO READ

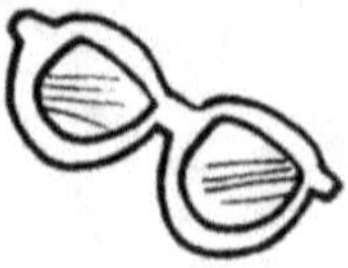

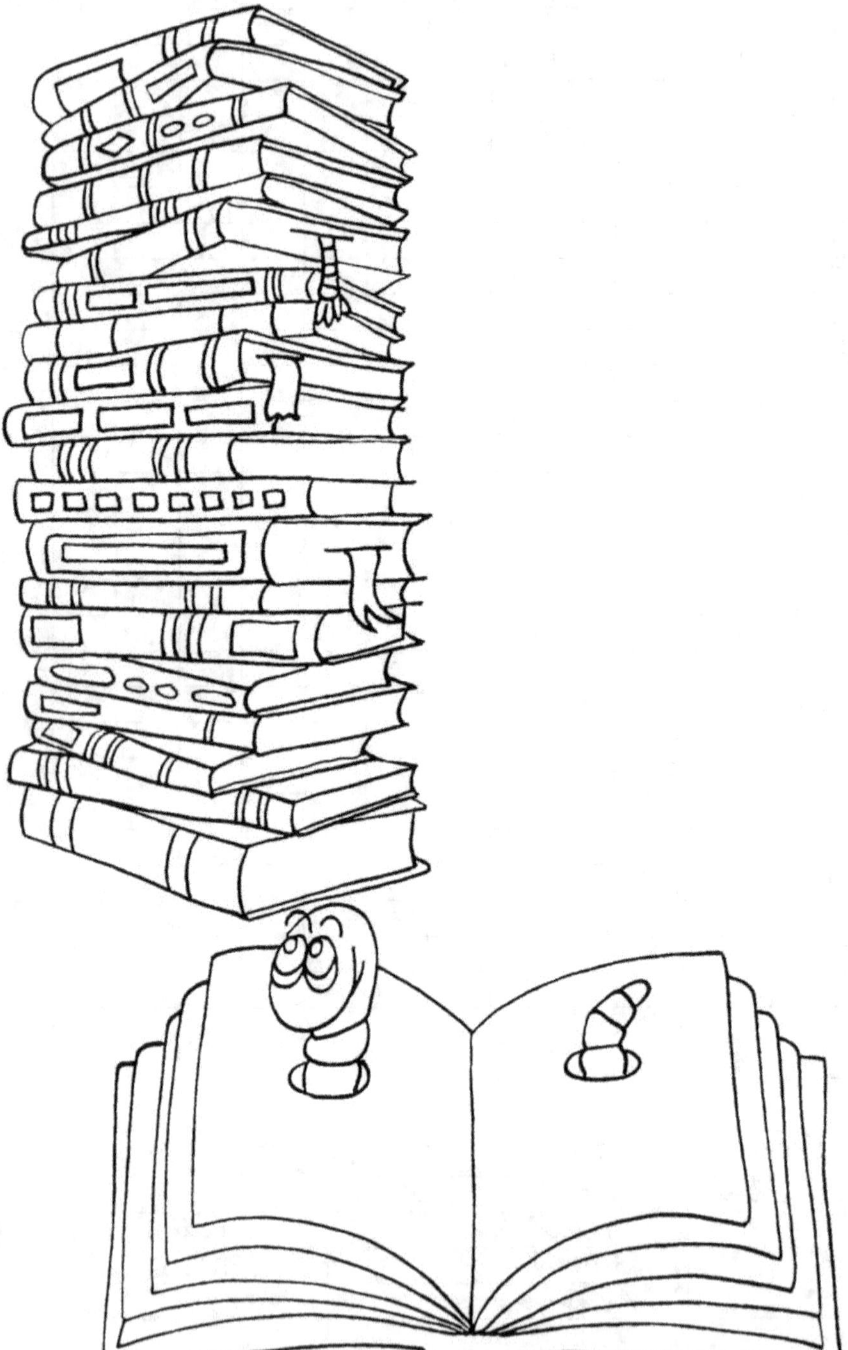

MOVIES TO WATCH

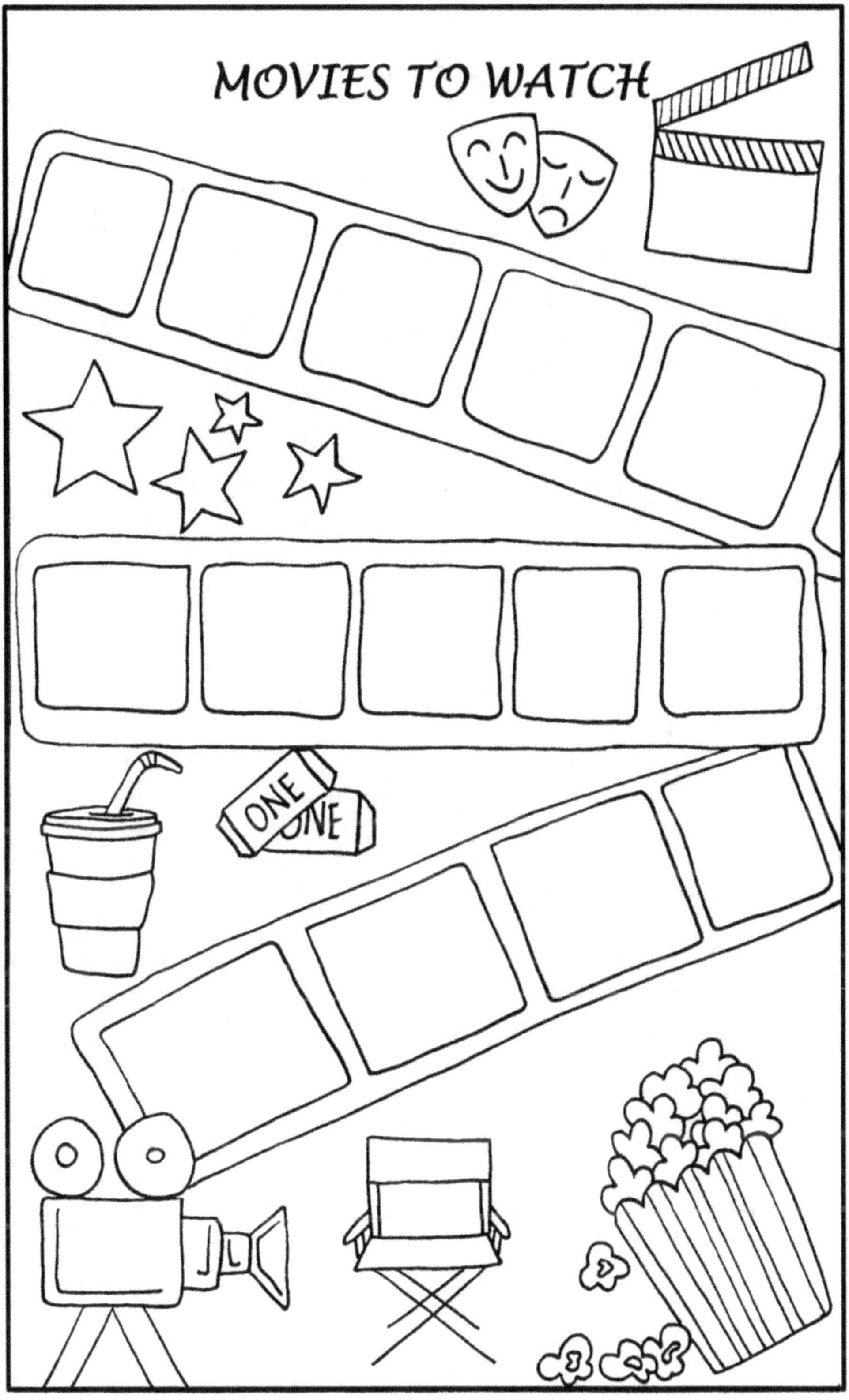

FITNESS LOG

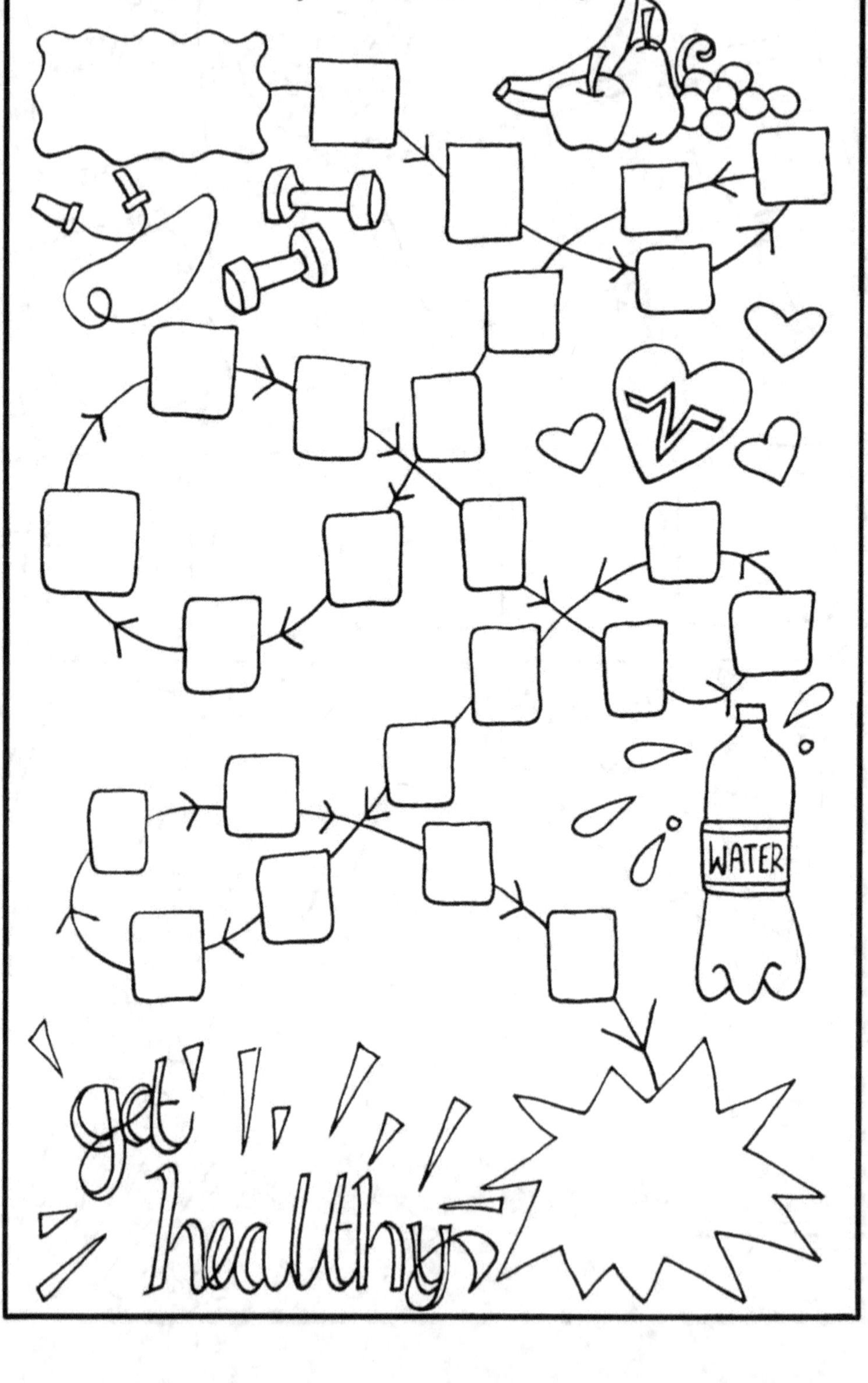

TRAVEL DREAMS

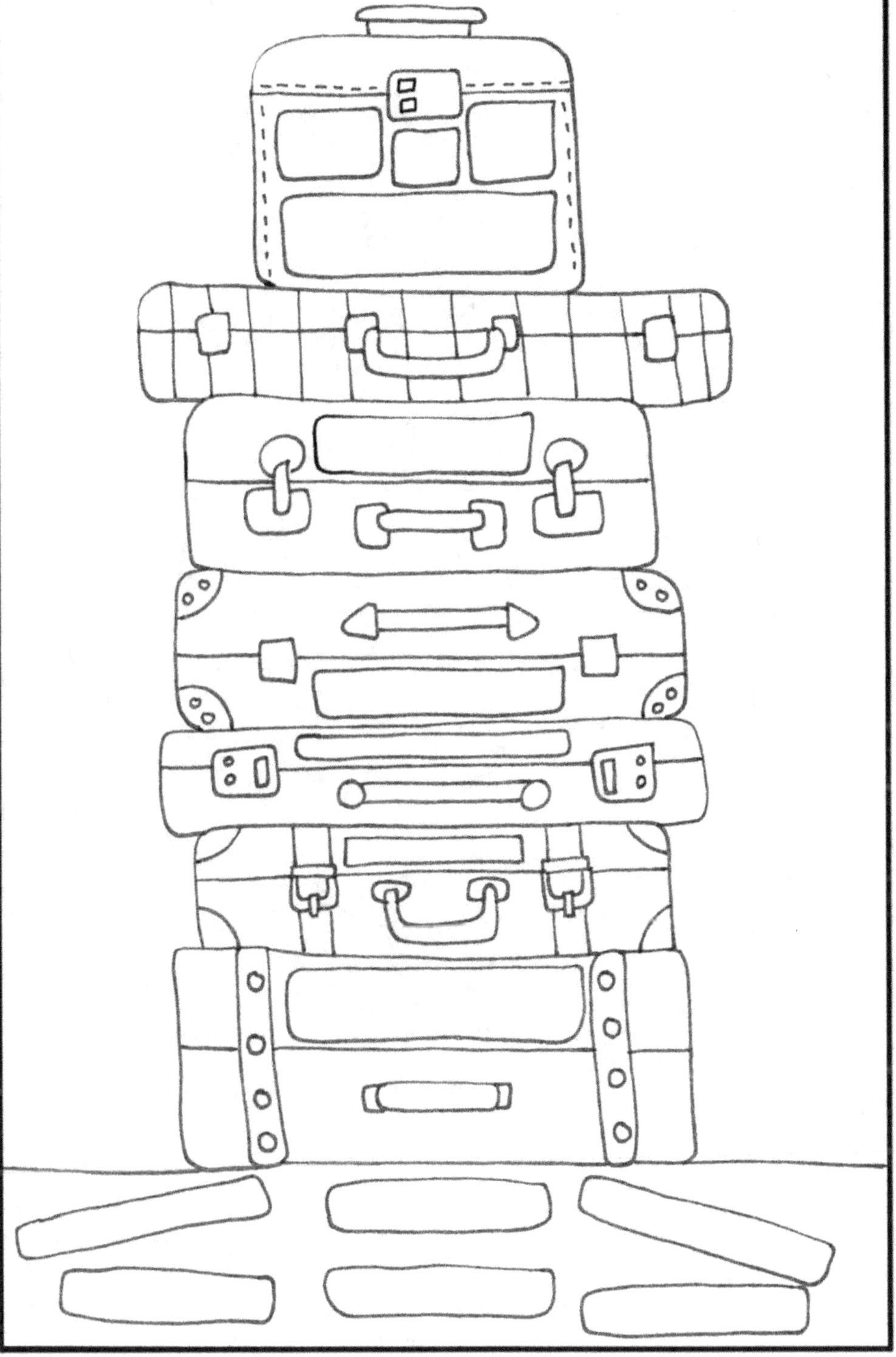

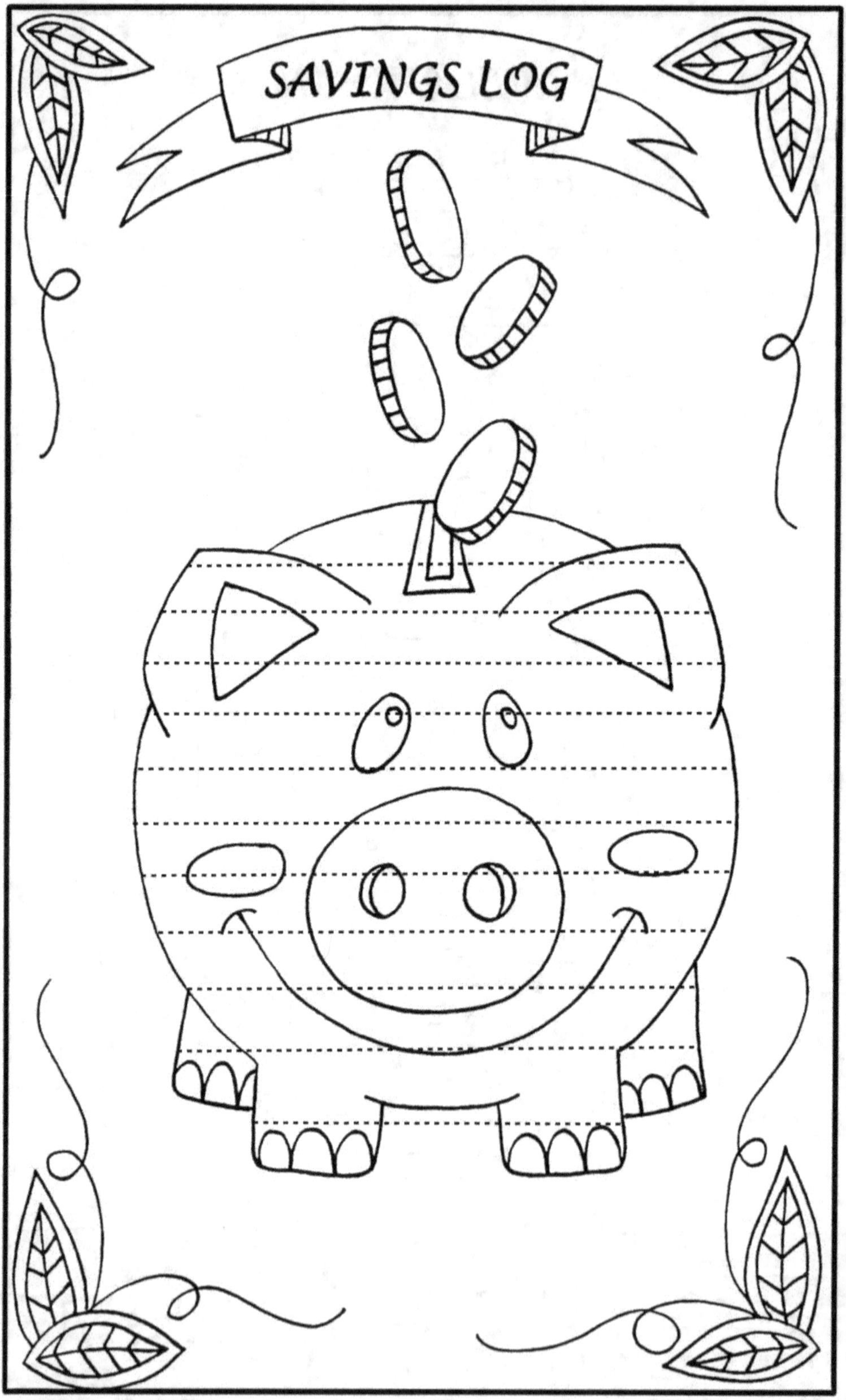
SAVINGS LOG

BUCKET LIST

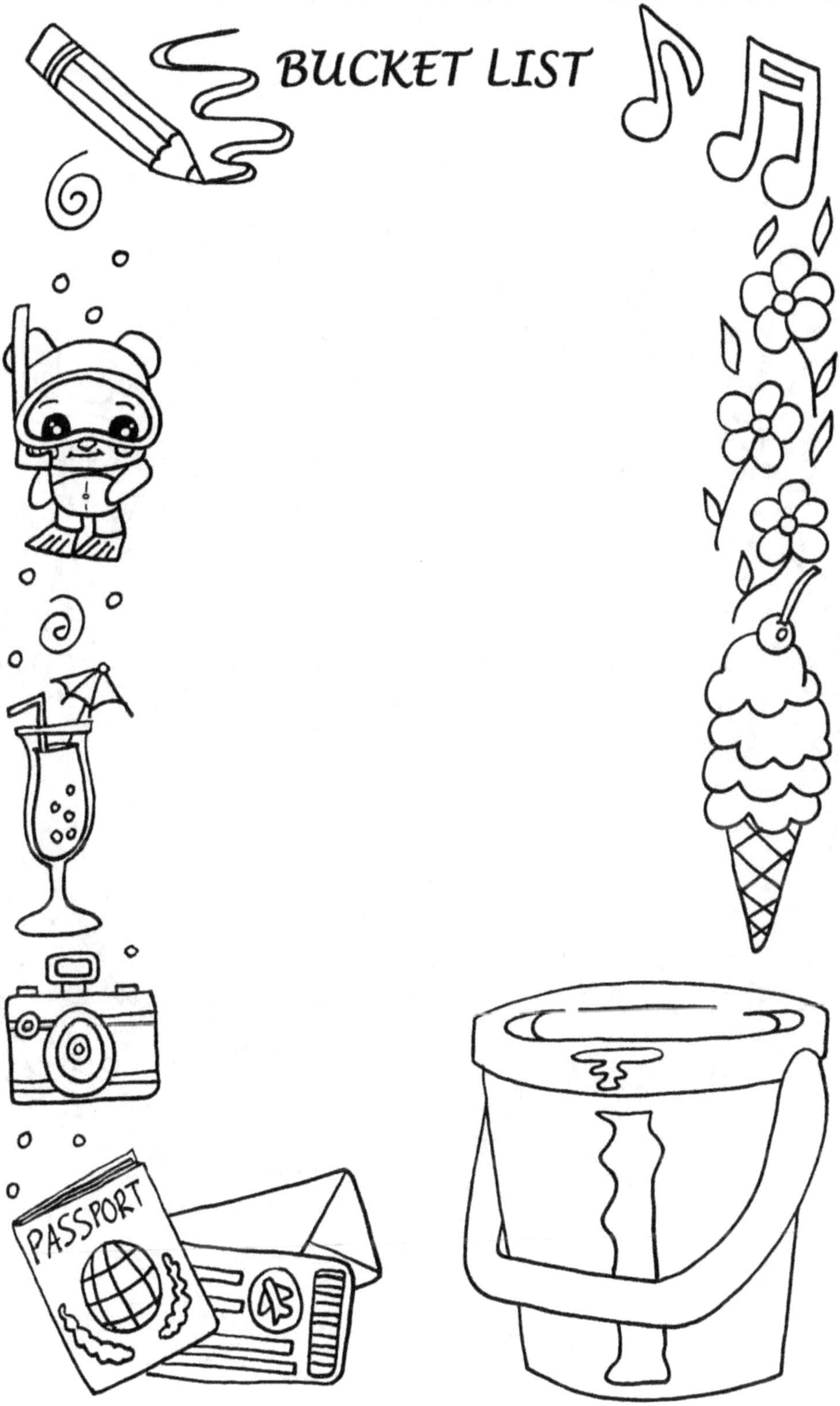

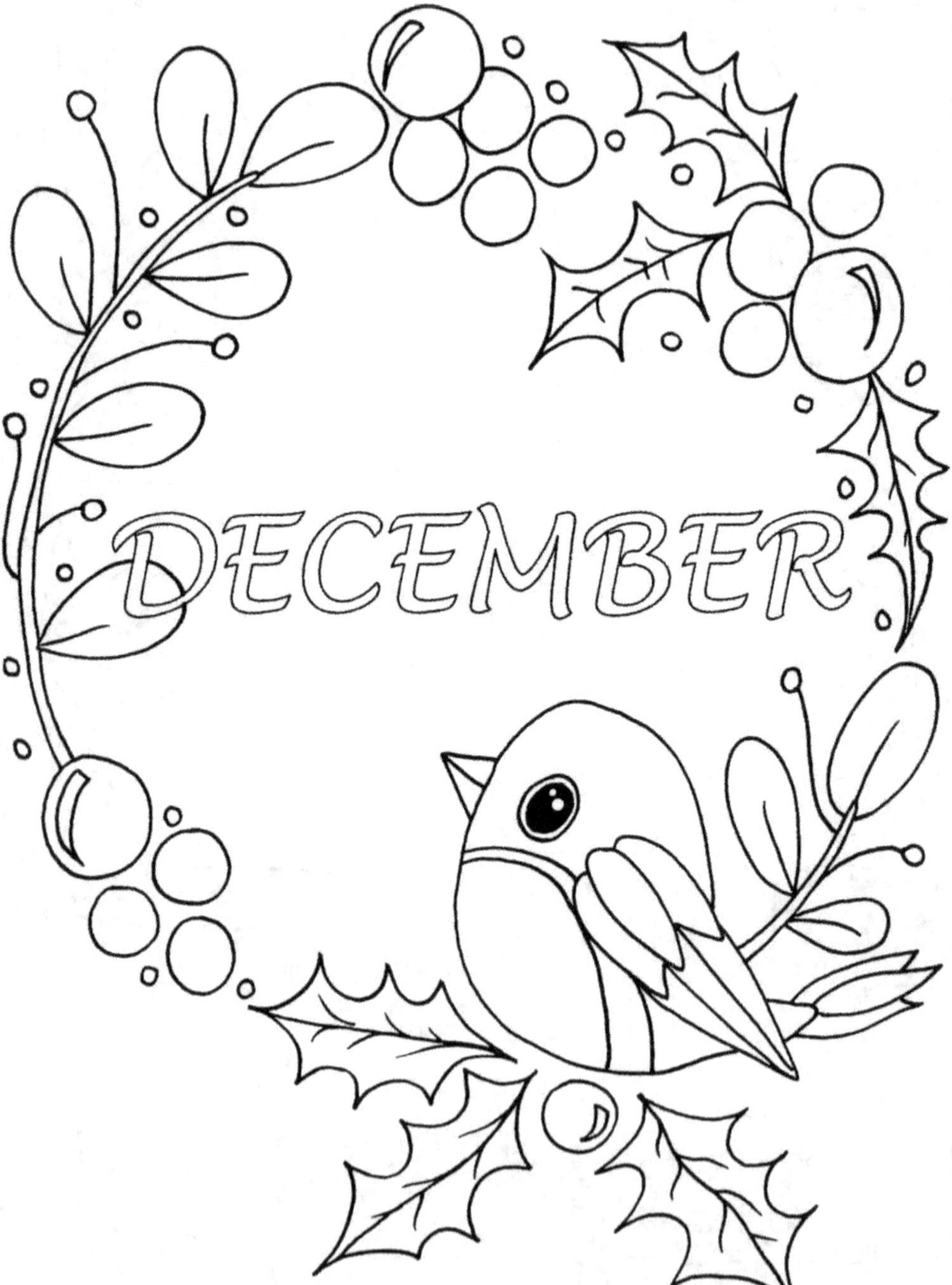
DECEMBER

Month at a glance ...

December

M	T	W	T	F	S	S

December To Do:

- ○ ________________________________
- ○ ________________________________
- ○ ________________________________
- ○ ________________________________
- ○ ________________________________
- ○ ________________________________
- ○ ________________________________
- ○ ________________________________
- ○ ________________________________

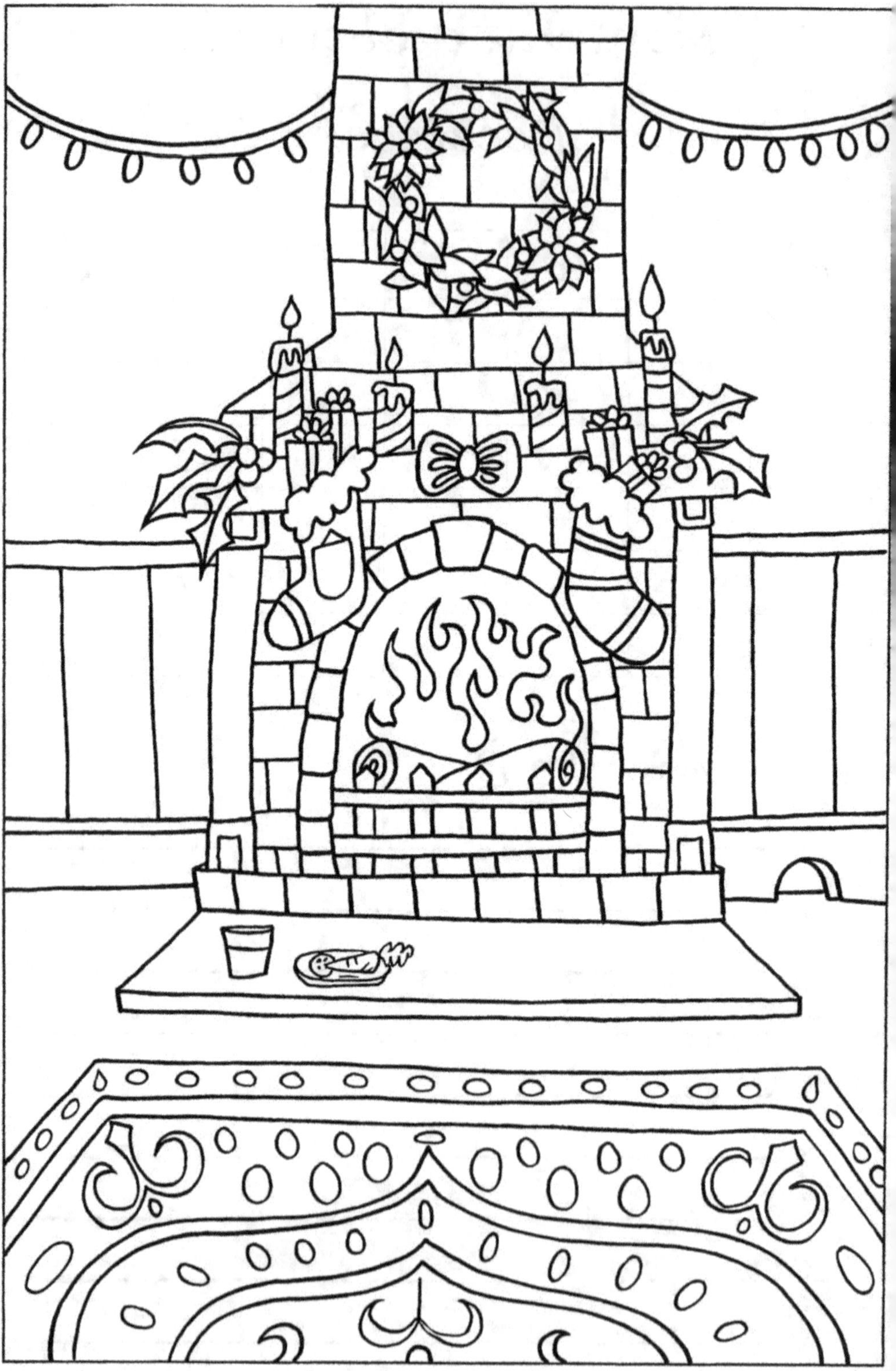

December

WEEK ______

M	T	W	T	F	S	S

Monday
Tuesday
Wednesday
Thursday
Friday
Saturday
Sunday
Notes

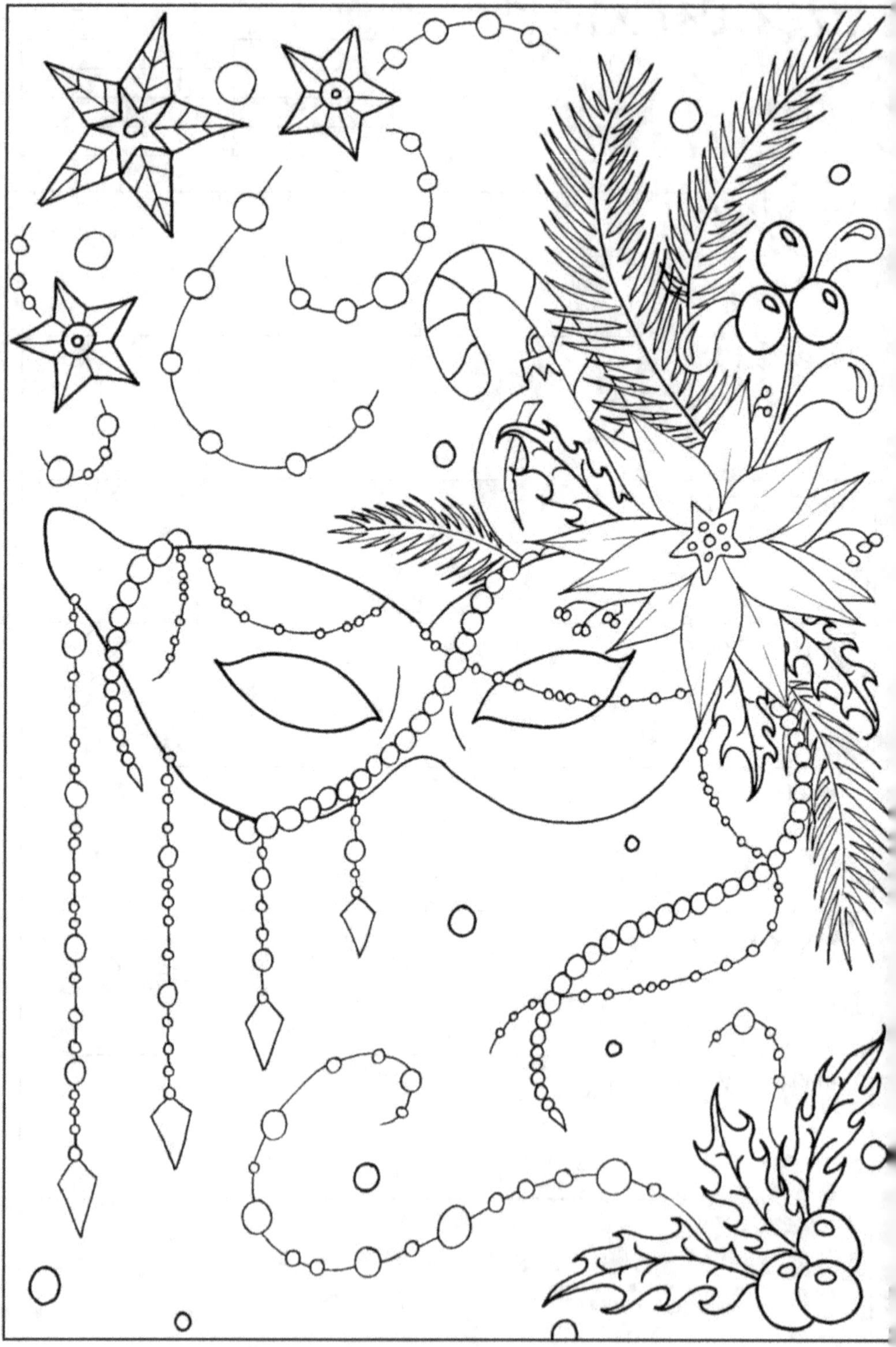

December

WEEK ______

M	T	W	T	F	S	S

Monday
Tuesday
Wednesday
Thursday
Friday
Saturday
Sunday
Notes

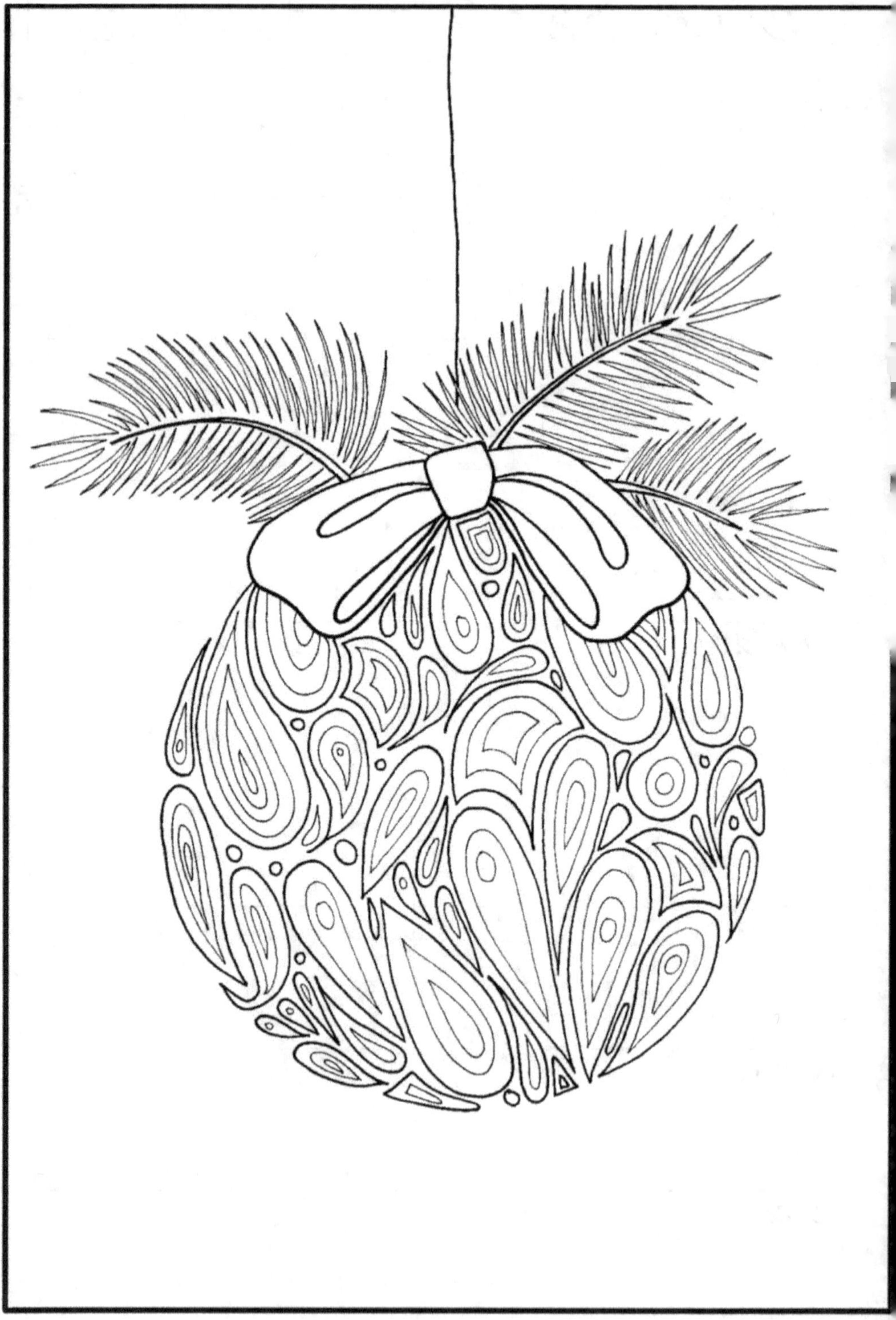

December

WEEK ______

M	T	W	T	F	S	S

Monday

Tuesday

Wednesday

Thursday

Friday

Saturday

Sunday

Notes

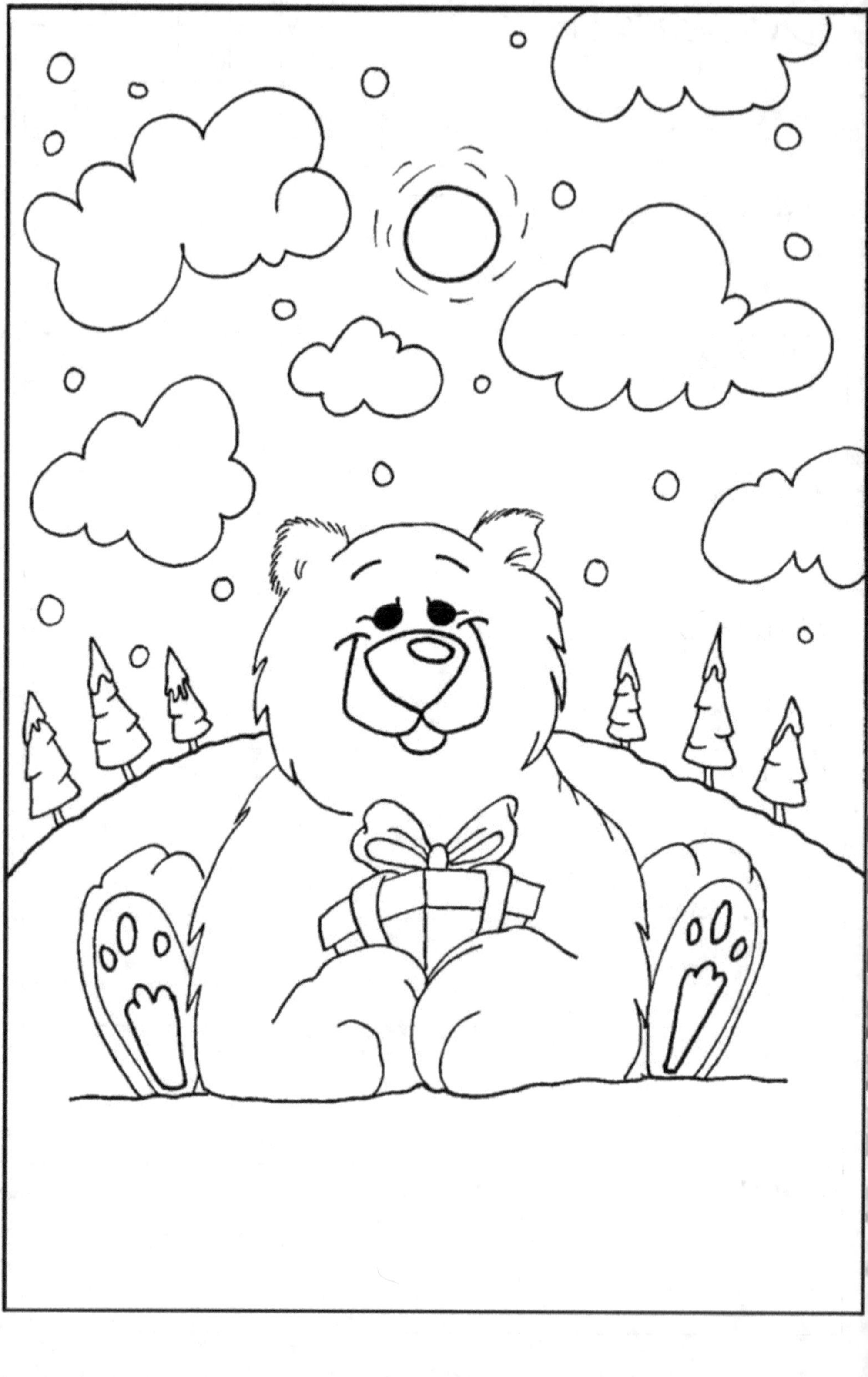

December

WEEK ______

M	T	W	T	F	S	S

Monday

Tuesday

Wednesday

Thursday

Friday

Saturday

Sunday

Notes

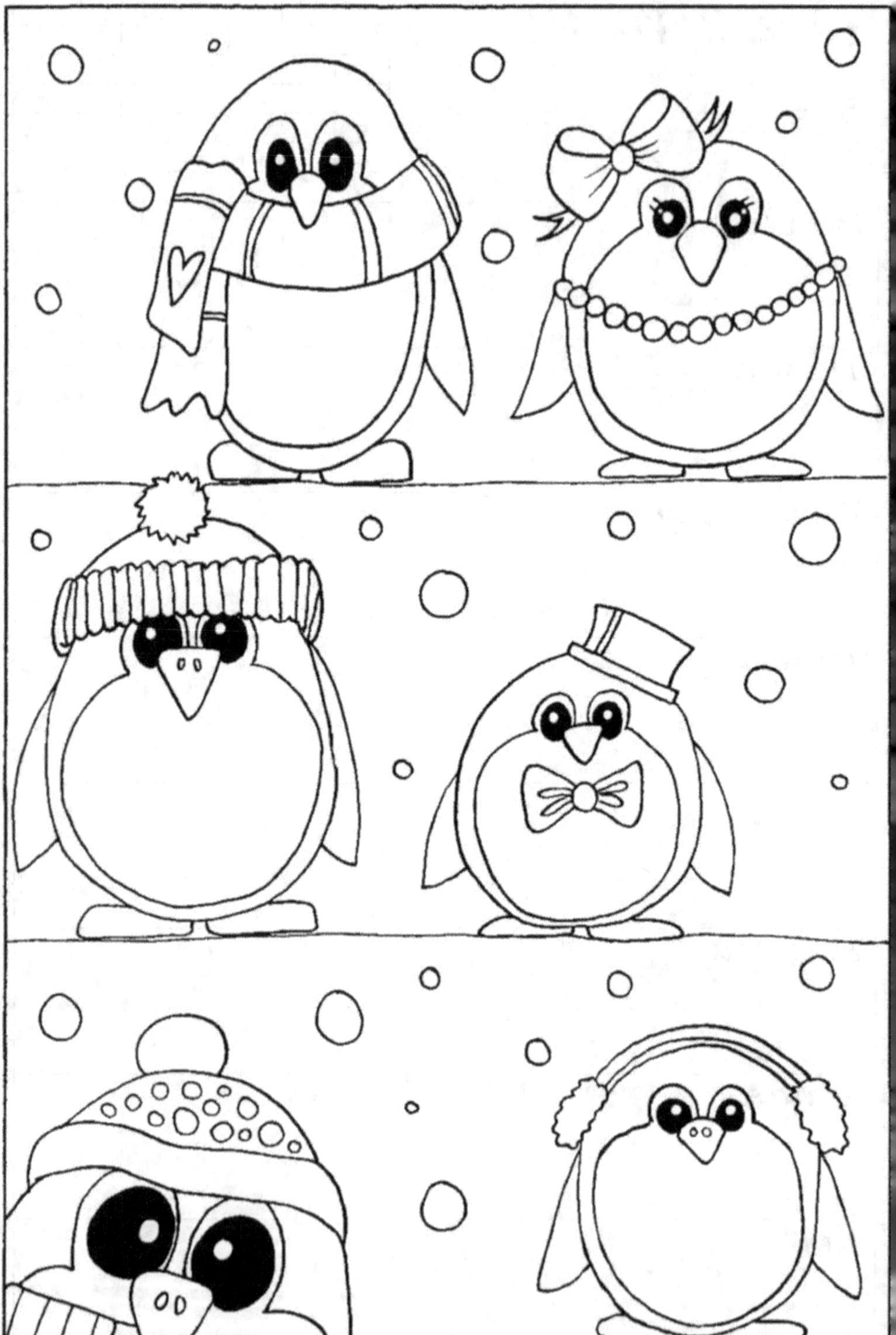

December

WEEK ______

M	T	W	T	F	S	S

Monday

Tuesday

Wednesday

Thursday

Friday

Saturday

Sunday

Notes

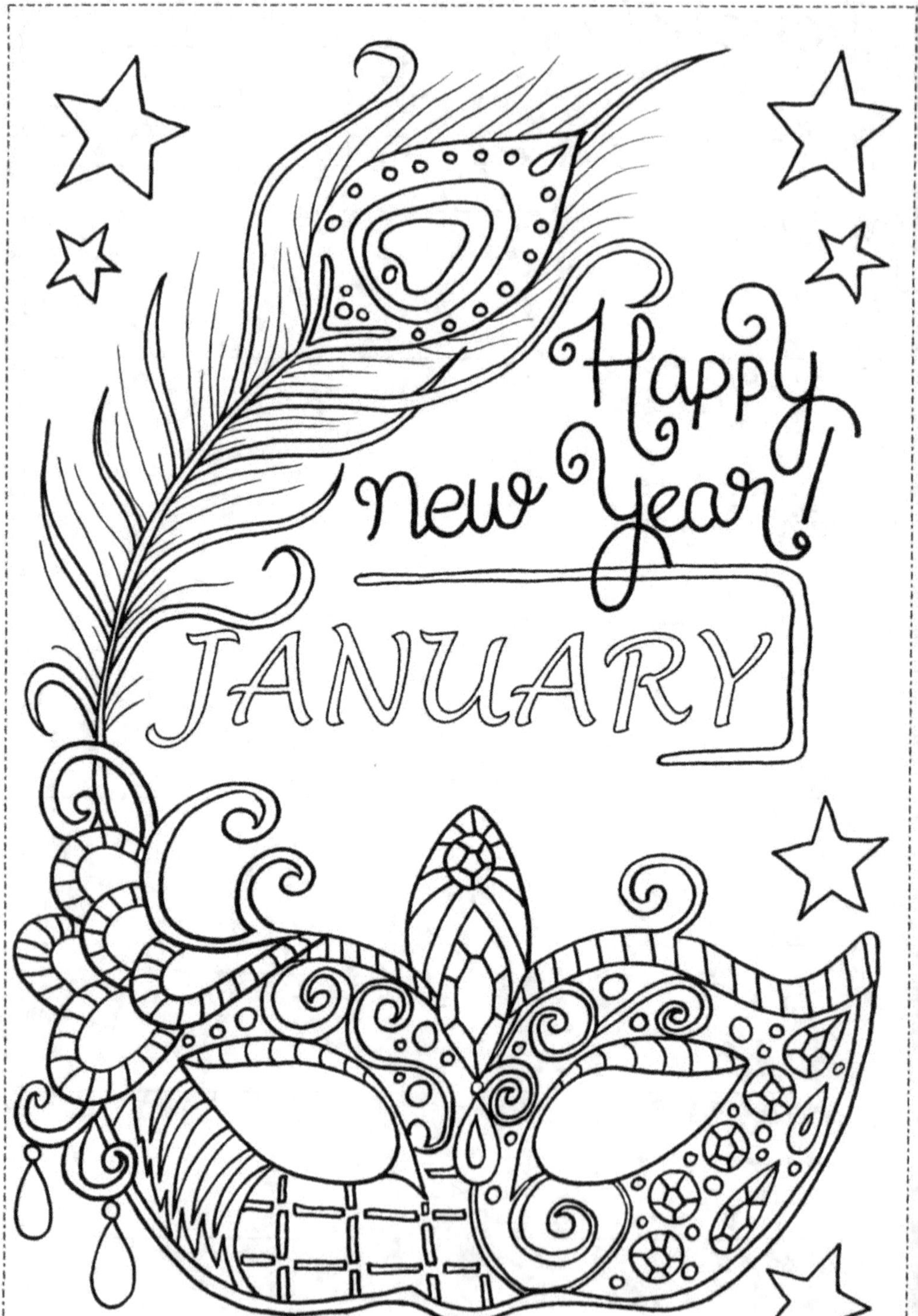
Happy new Year!
JANUARY

Month at a glance …

January

M	T	W	T	F	S	S

January To Do:

- ○ ________________________________
- ○ ________________________________
- ○ ________________________________
- ○ ________________________________
- ○ ________________________________
- ○ ________________________________
- ○ ________________________________
- ○ ________________________________
- ○ ________________________________

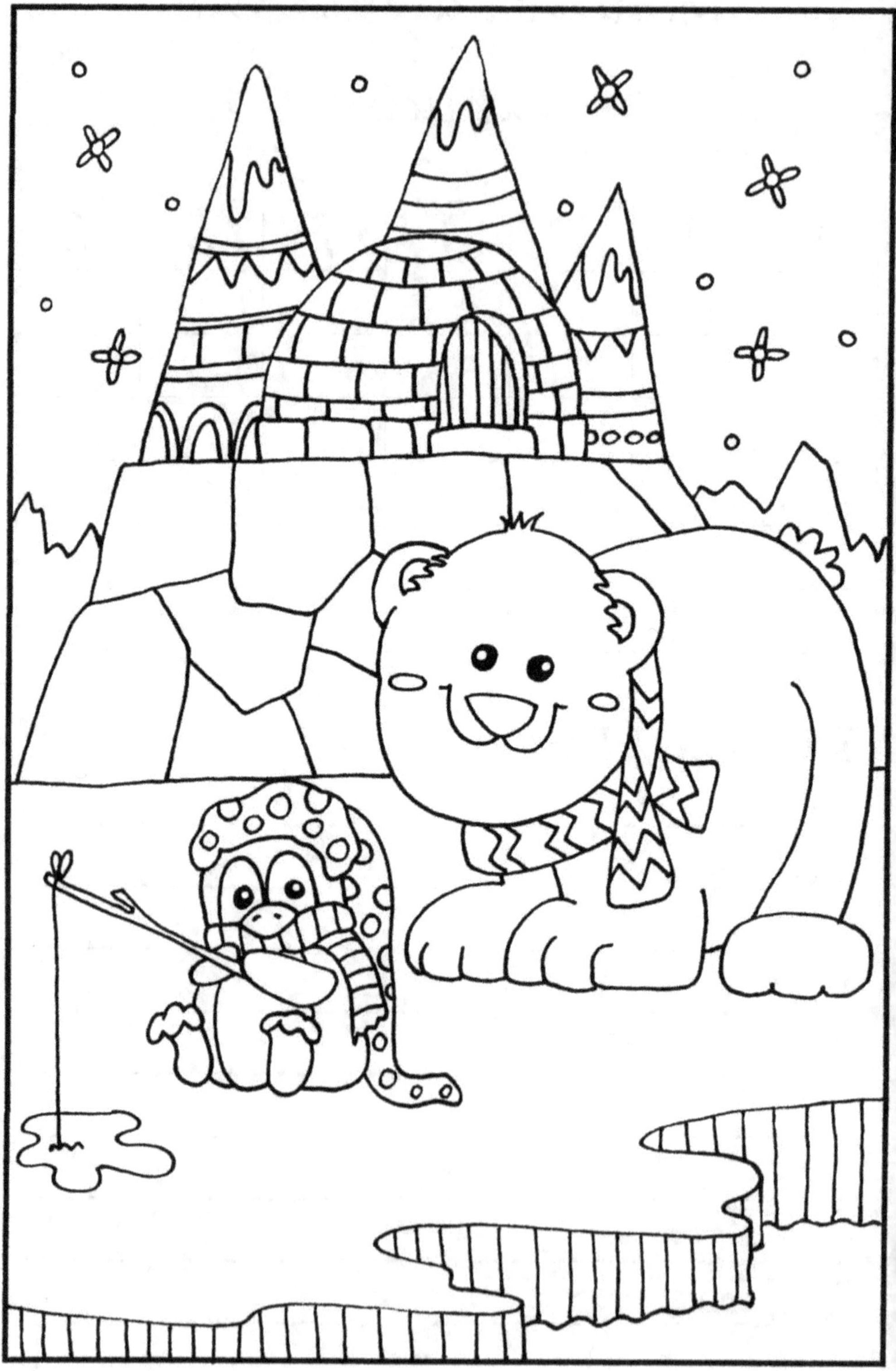

January

WEEK ______

M	T	W	T	F	S	S

Monday

Tuesday

Wednesday

Thursday

Friday

Saturday

Sunday

Notes

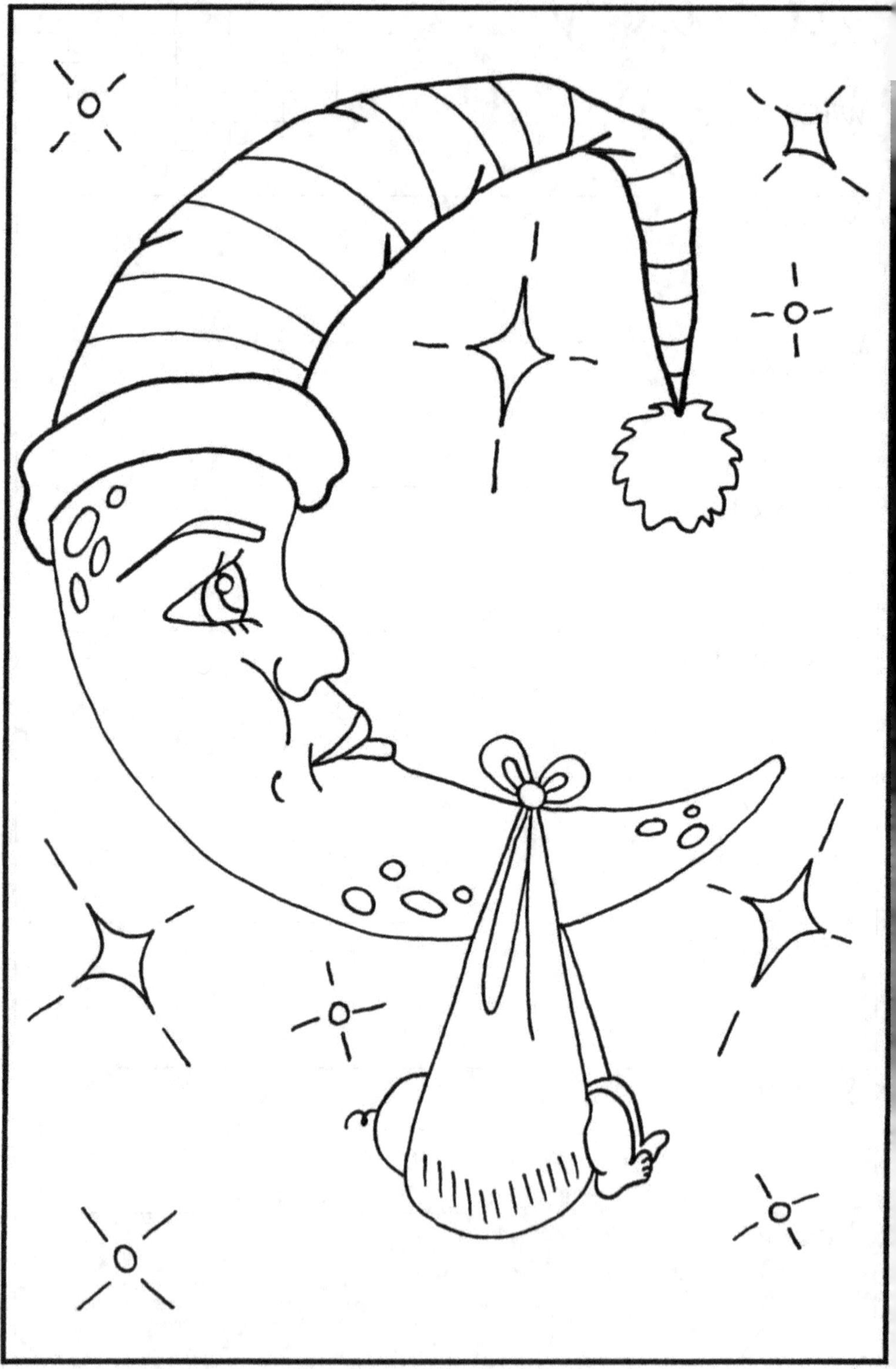

January

WEEK ______

M	T	W	T	F	S	S

Monday
Tuesday
Wednesday
Thursday
Friday
Saturday
Sunday
Notes

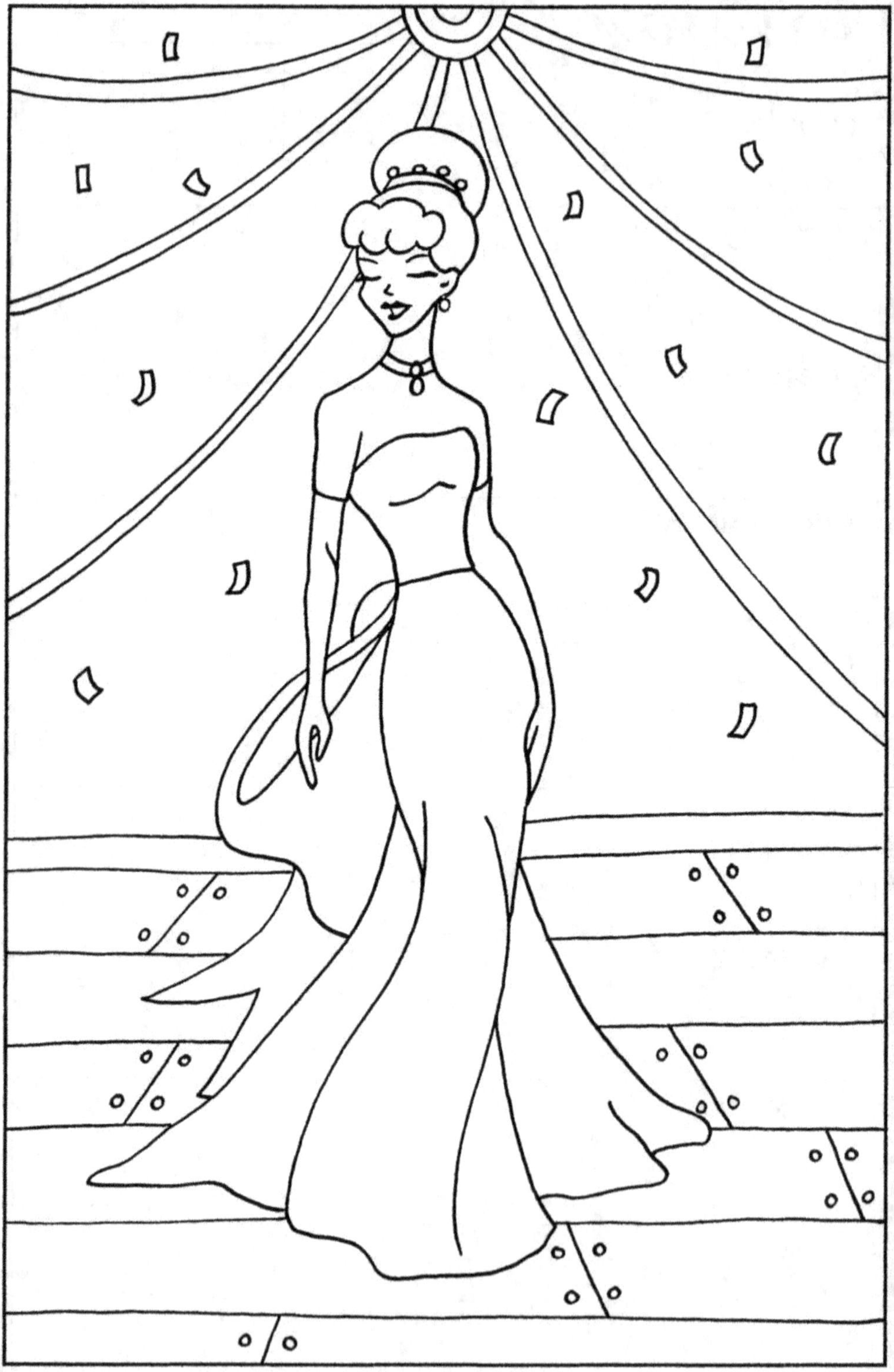

January

WEEK ______

M	T	W	T	F	S	S

Monday

Tuesday

Wednesday

Thursday

Friday

Saturday

Sunday

Notes

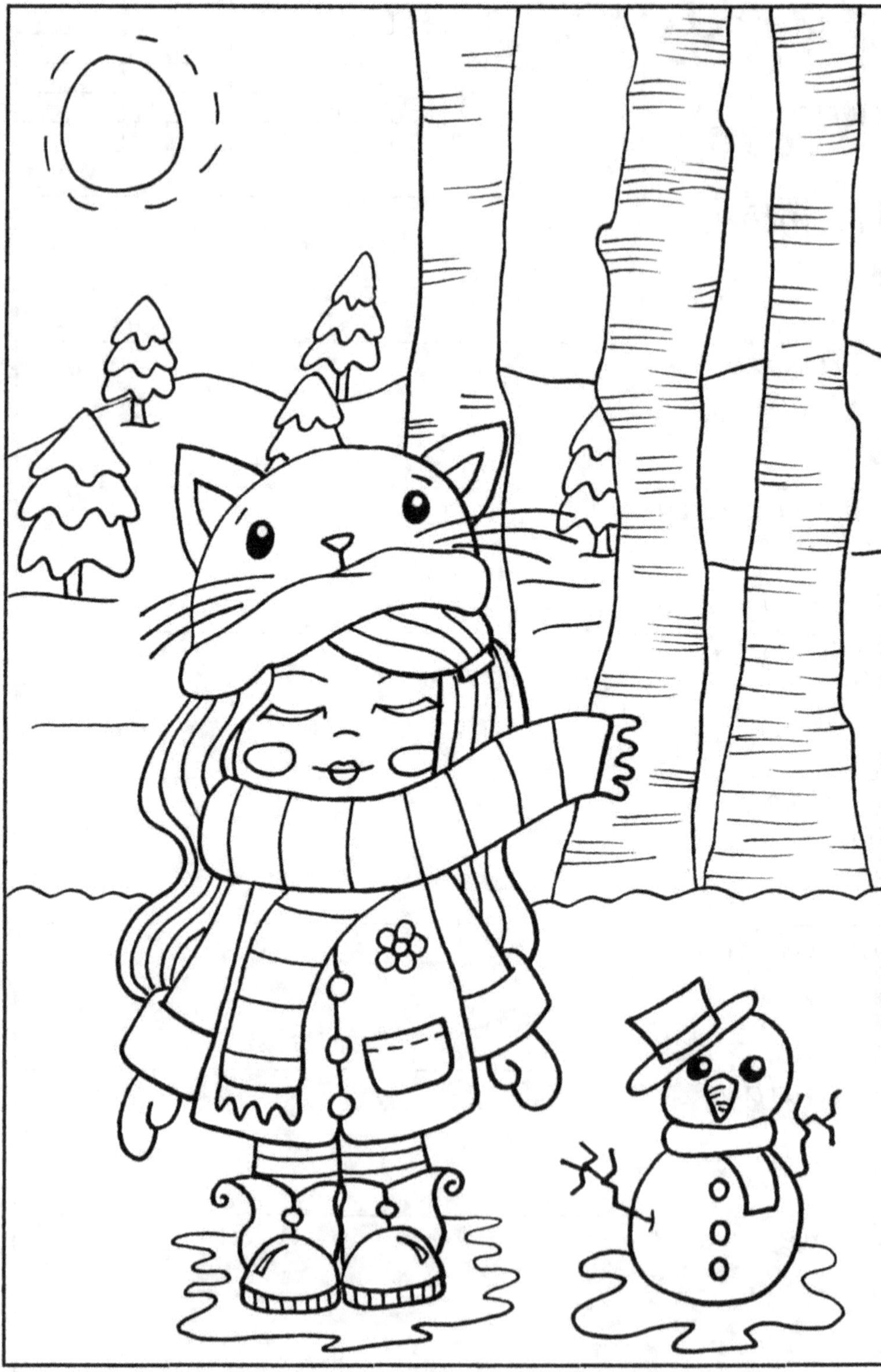

January

WEEK ______

M	T	W	T	F	S	S

Monday

Tuesday

Wednesday

Thursday

Friday

Saturday

Sunday

Notes

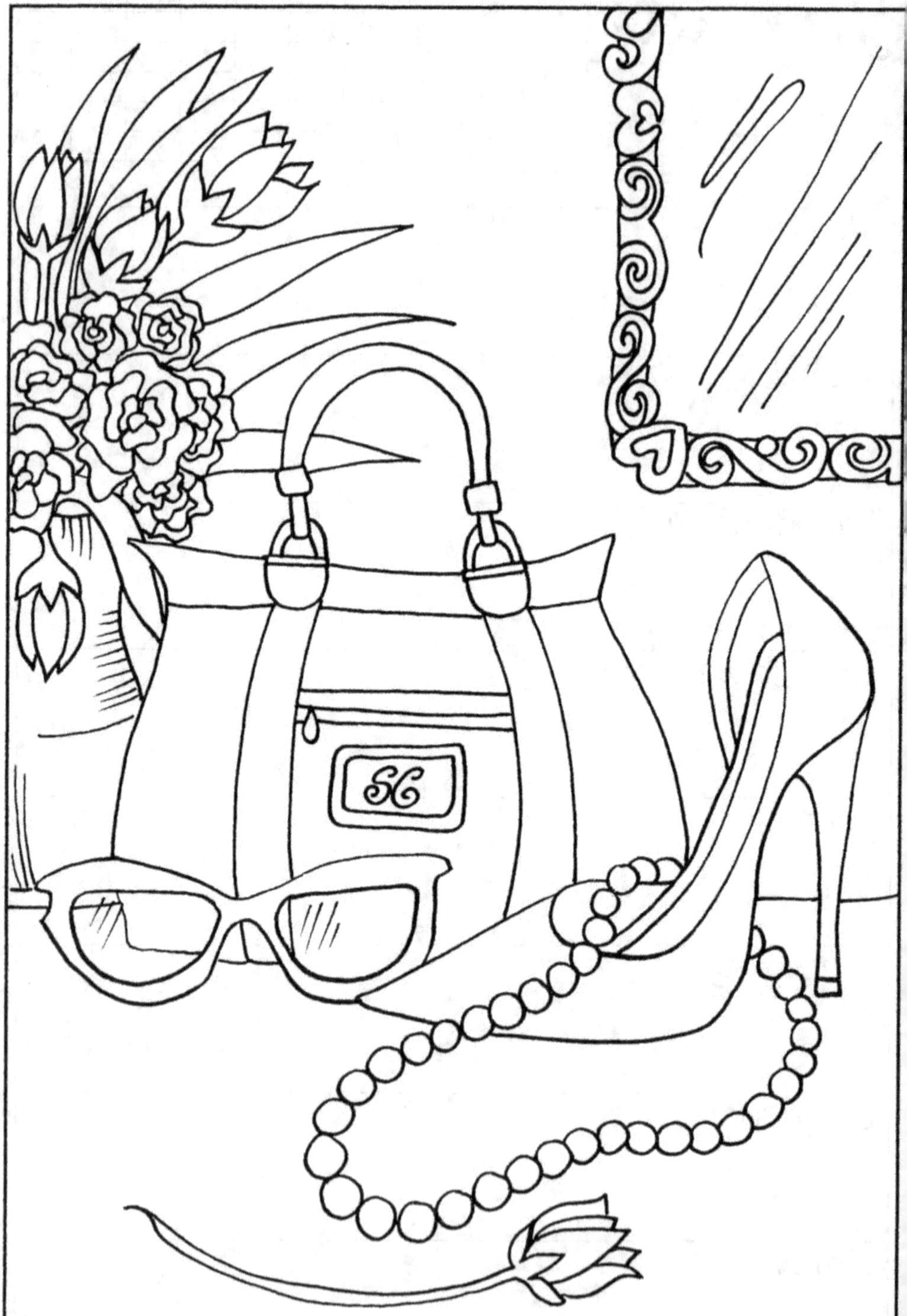

January

WEEK ______

M	T	W	T	F	S	S

Monday

Tuesday

Wednesday

Thursday

Friday

Saturday

Sunday

Notes

FEBRUARY

Month at a glance …

February

M	T	W	T	F	S	S

February To Do:

- ○ ______________________________
- ○ ______________________________
- ○ ______________________________
- ○ ______________________________
- ○ ______________________________
- ○ ______________________________
- ○ ______________________________
- ○ ______________________________
- ○ ______________________________

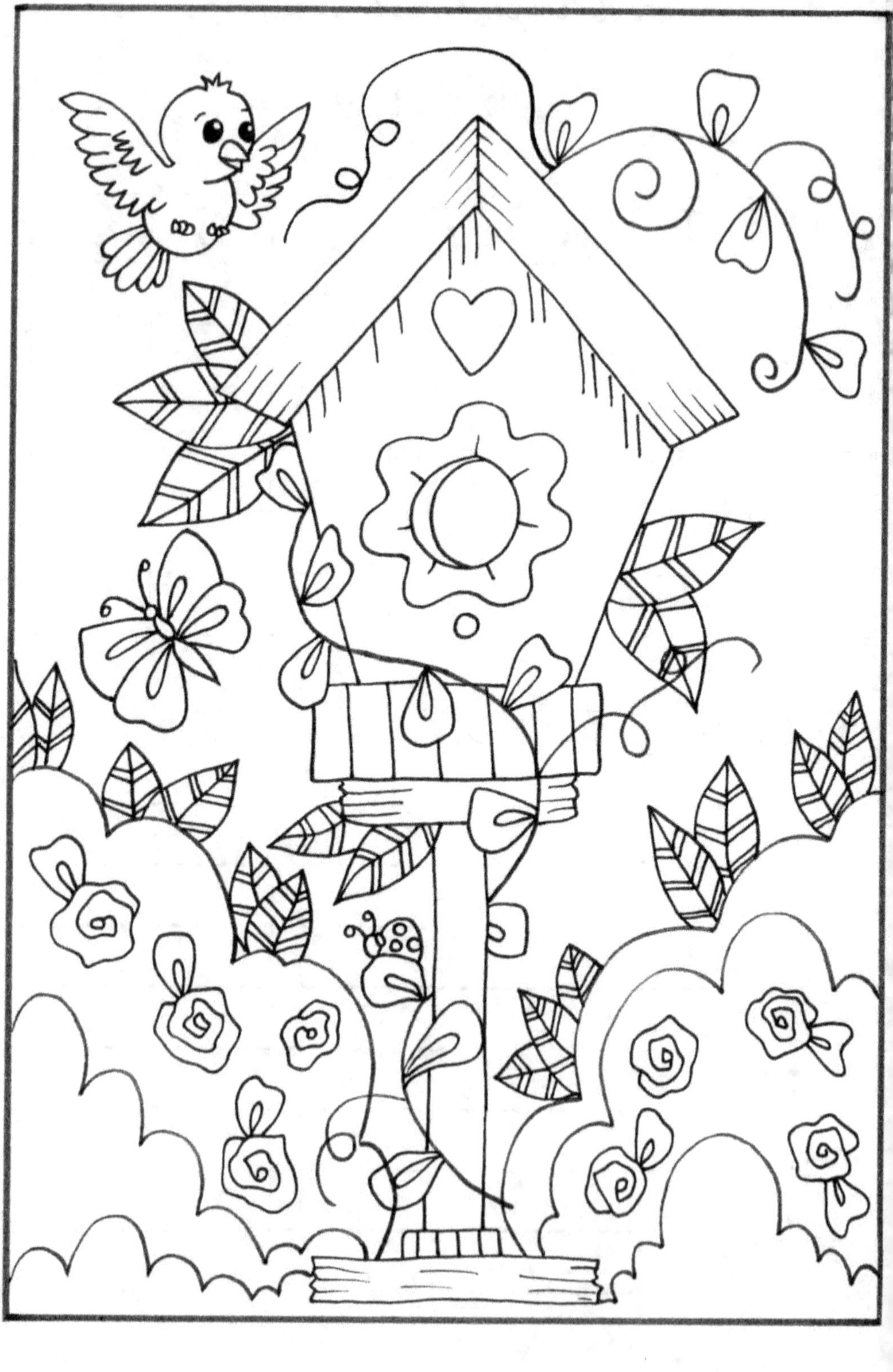

February

WEEK ______

M	T	W	T	F	S	S

Monday

Tuesday

Wednesday

Thursday

Friday

Saturday

Sunday

Notes

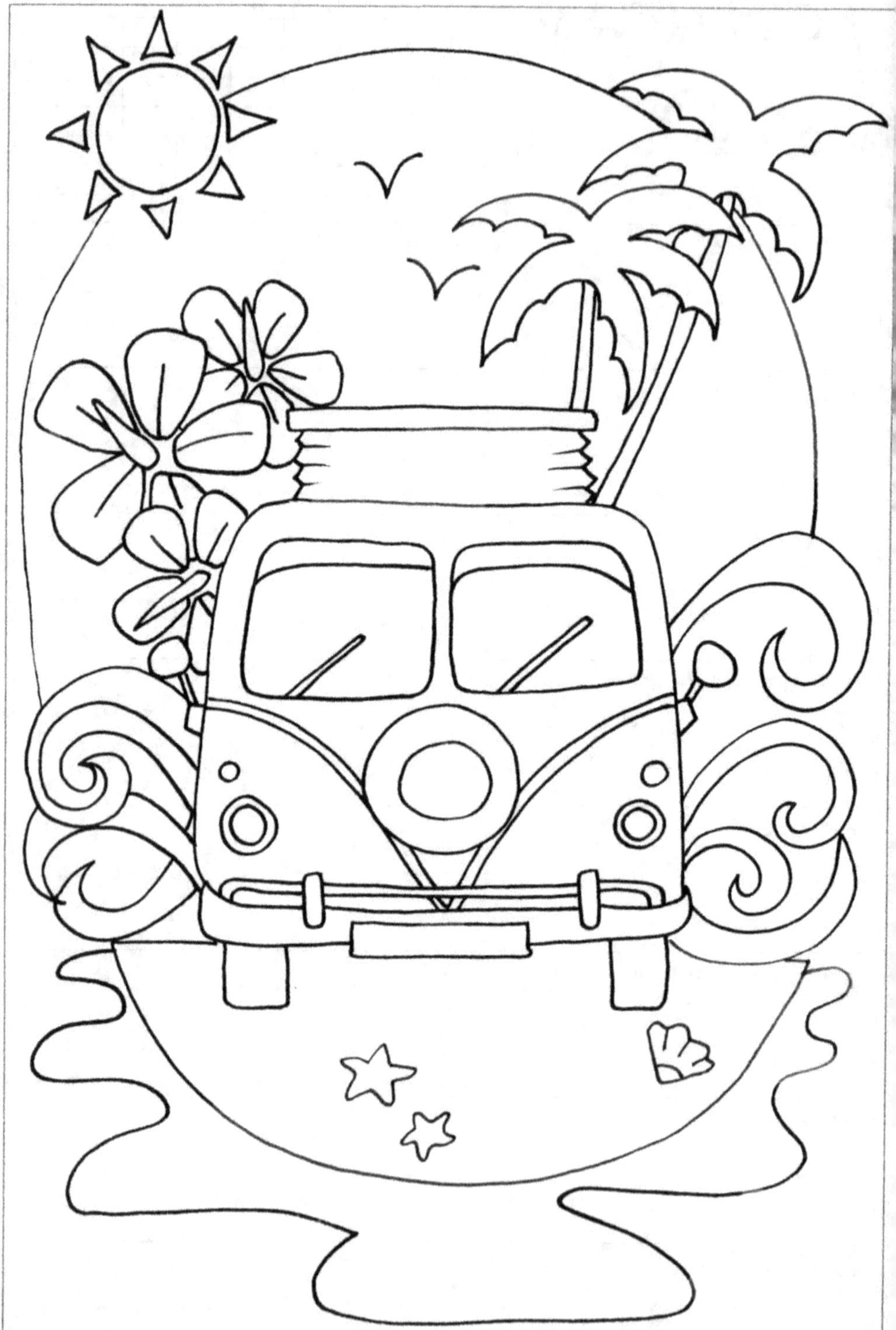

February

M	T	W	T	F	S	S

WEEK ______

Monday

Tuesday

Wednesday

Thursday

Friday

Saturday

Sunday

Notes

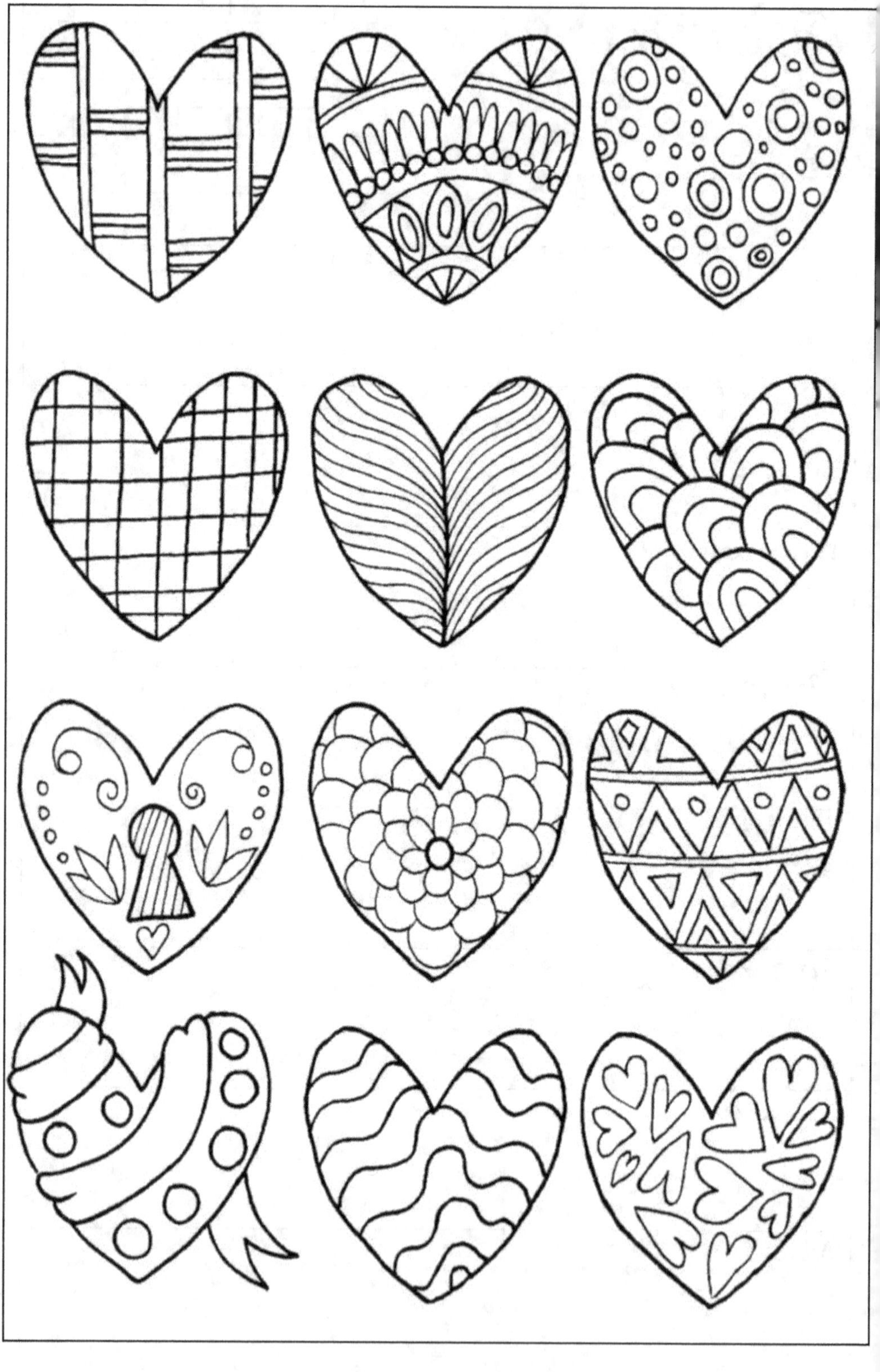

February

M	T	W	T	F	S	S

WEEK ______

Monday
Tuesday
Wednesday
Thursday
Friday
Saturday
Sunday
Notes

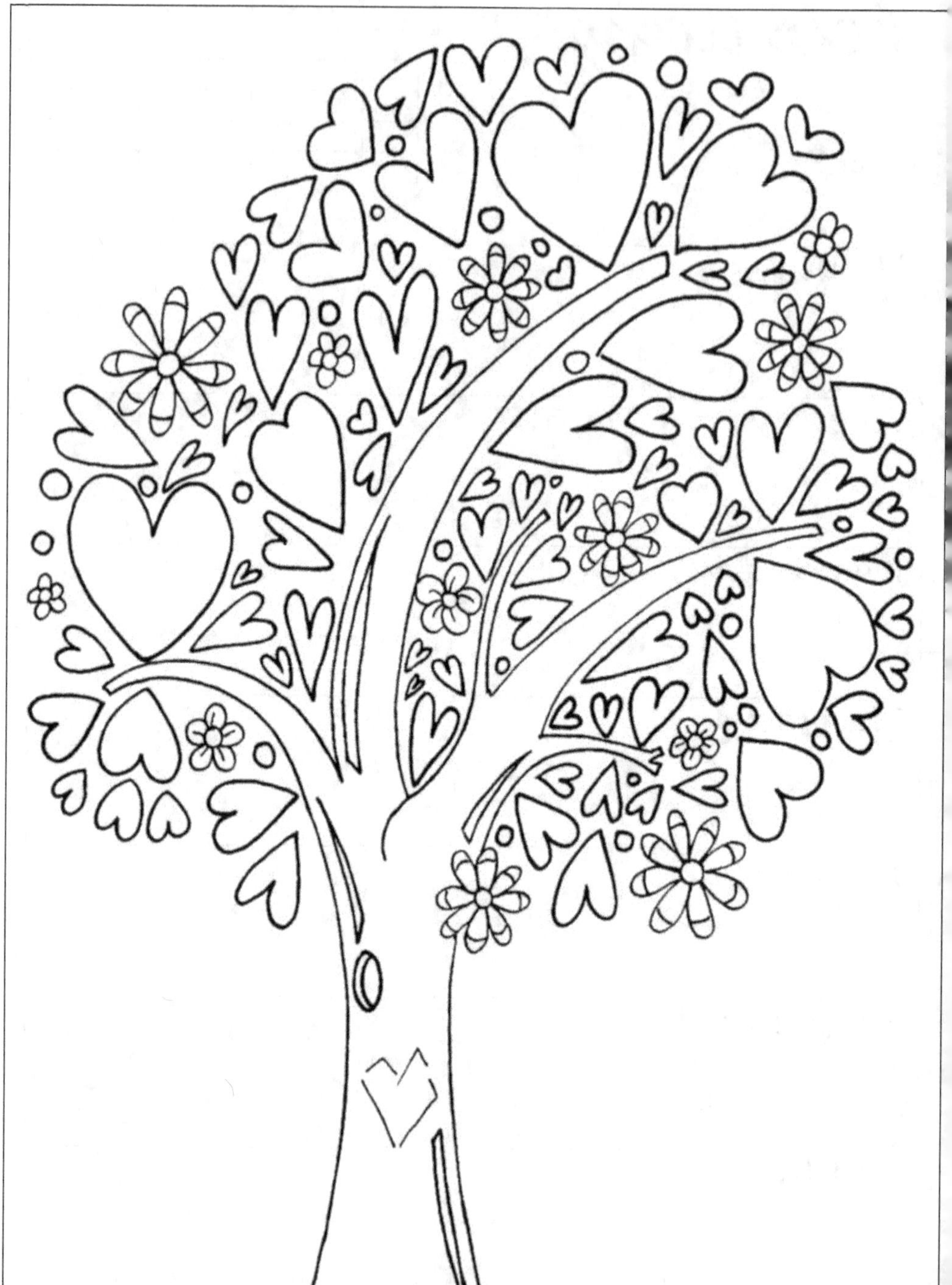

February

M	T	W	T	F	S	S

WEEK ______

Monday

Tuesday

Wednesday

Thursday

Friday

Saturday

Sunday

Notes

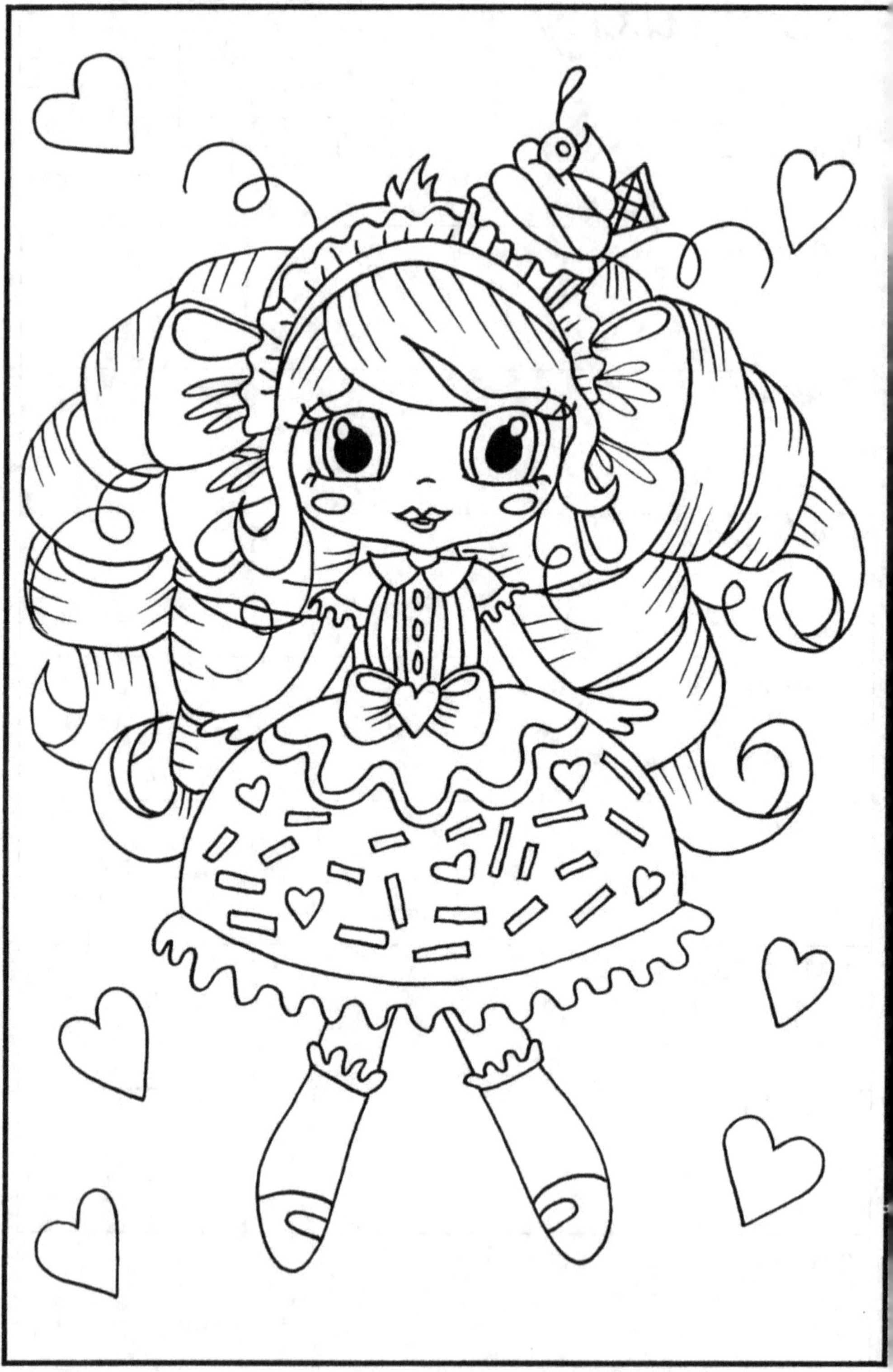

February

WEEK ______

M	T	W	T	F	S	S

Monday
Tuesday
Wednesday
Thursday
Friday
Saturday
Sunday
Notes

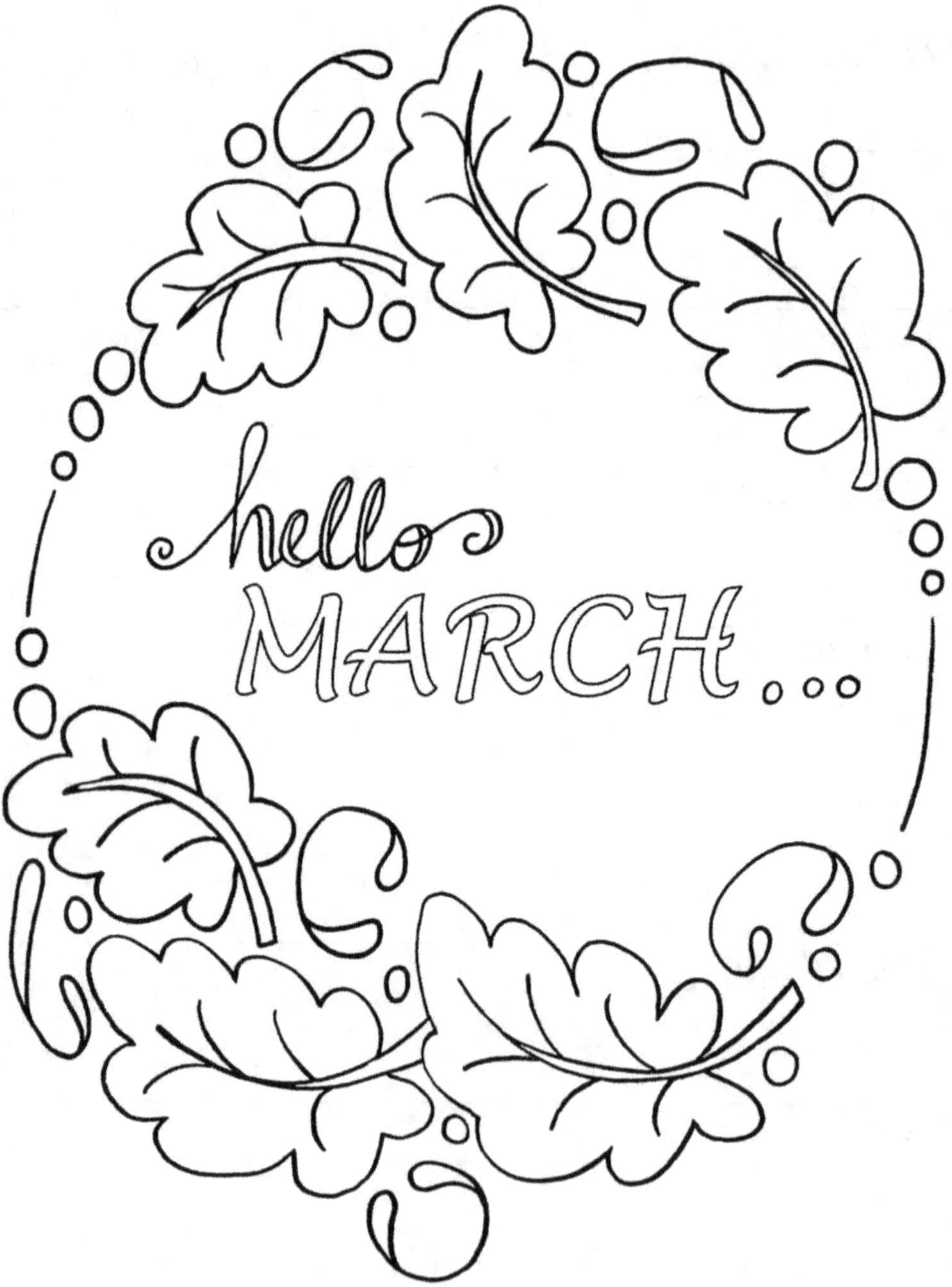
hello
MARCH...

Month at a glance …

March

M	T	W	T	F	S	S

March To Do:

- ○ ___________________________________
- ○ ___________________________________
- ○ ___________________________________
- ○ ___________________________________
- ○ ___________________________________
- ○ ___________________________________
- ○ ___________________________________
- ○ ___________________________________
- ○ ___________________________________

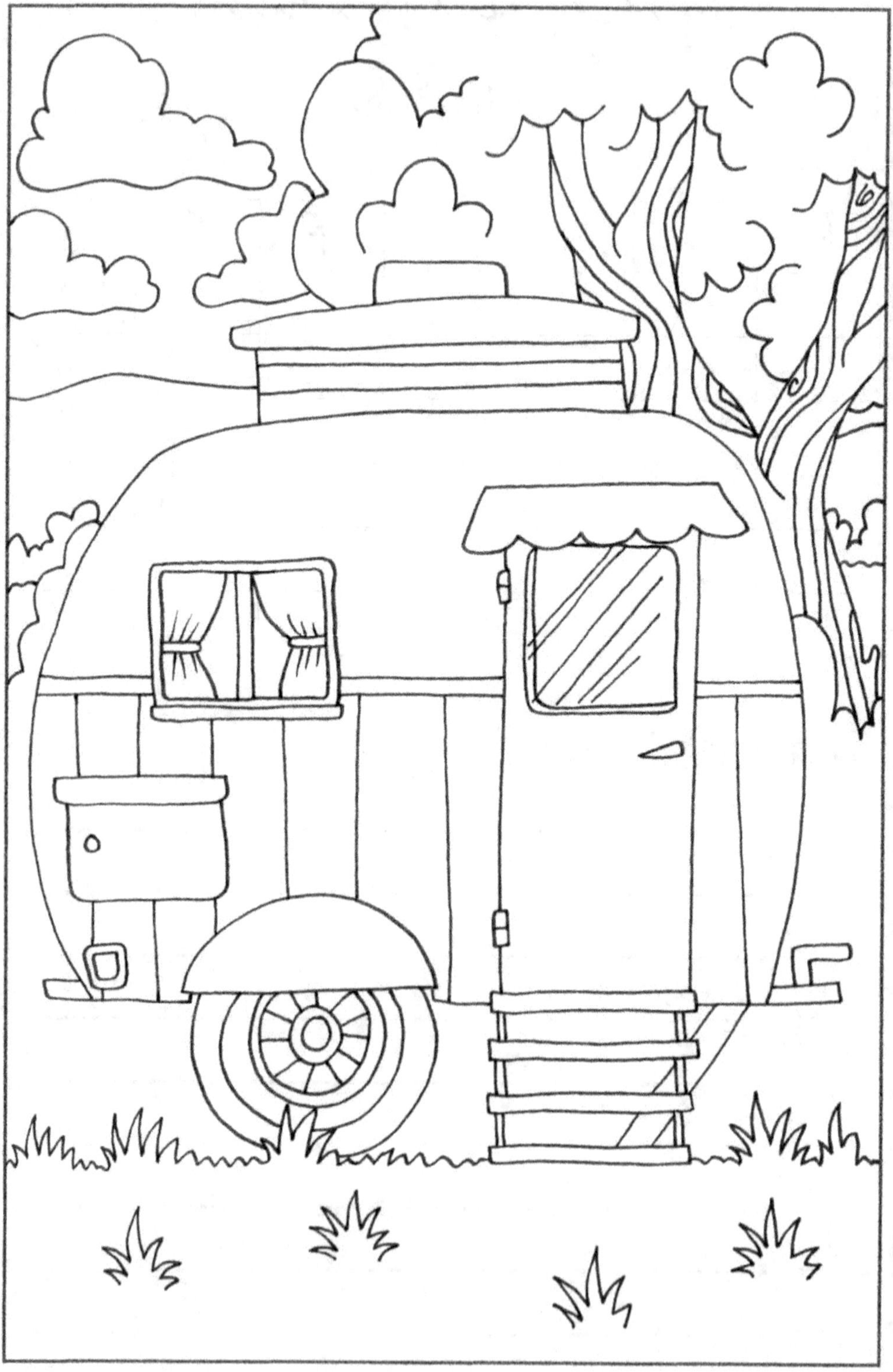

March

WEEK ______

M	T	W	T	F	S	S

Monday

Tuesday

Wednesday

Thursday

Friday

Saturday

Sunday

Notes

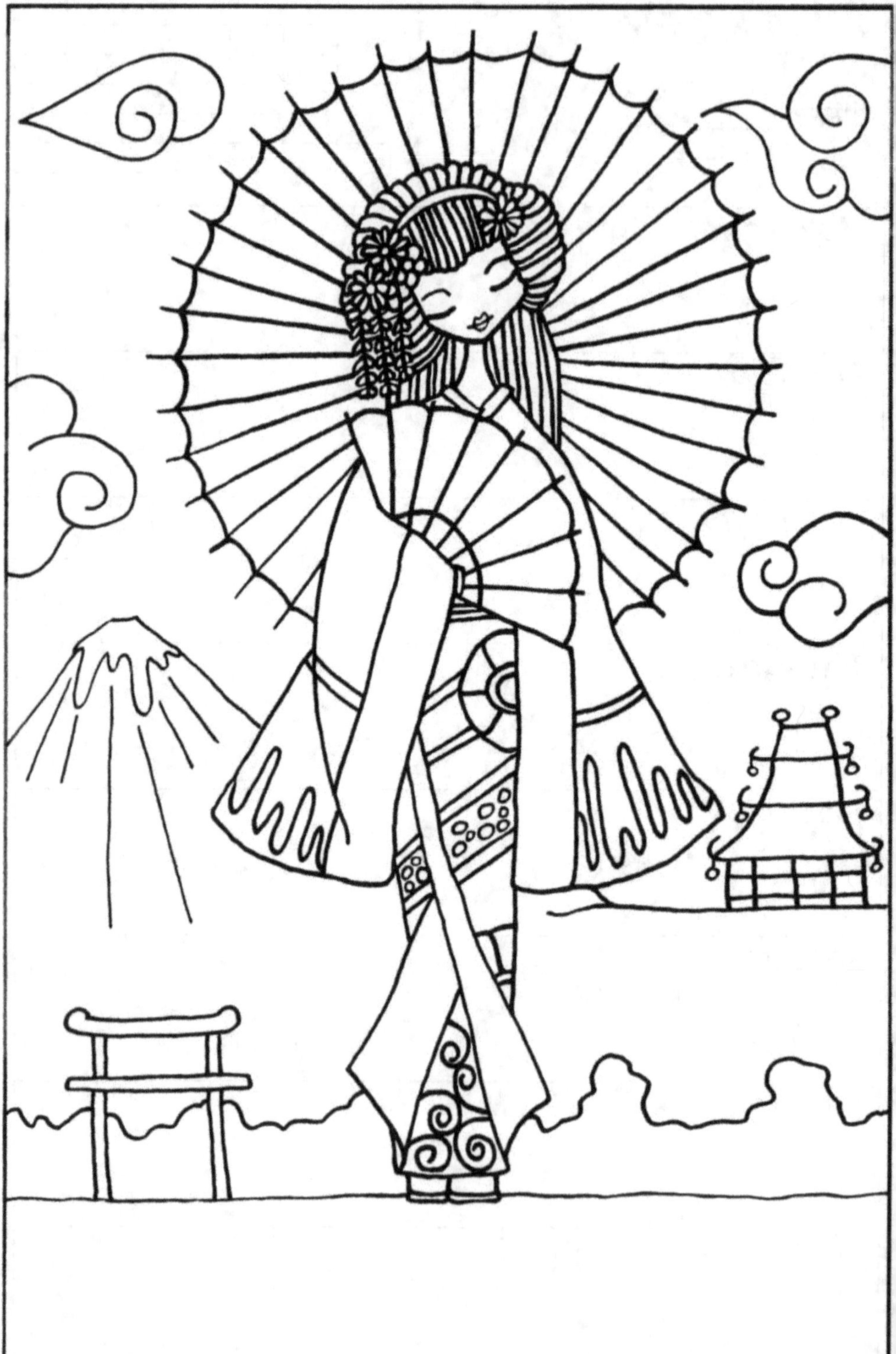

March

WEEK _____

M	T	W	T	F	S	S

Monday
Tuesday
Wednesday
Thursday
Friday
Saturday
Sunday
Notes

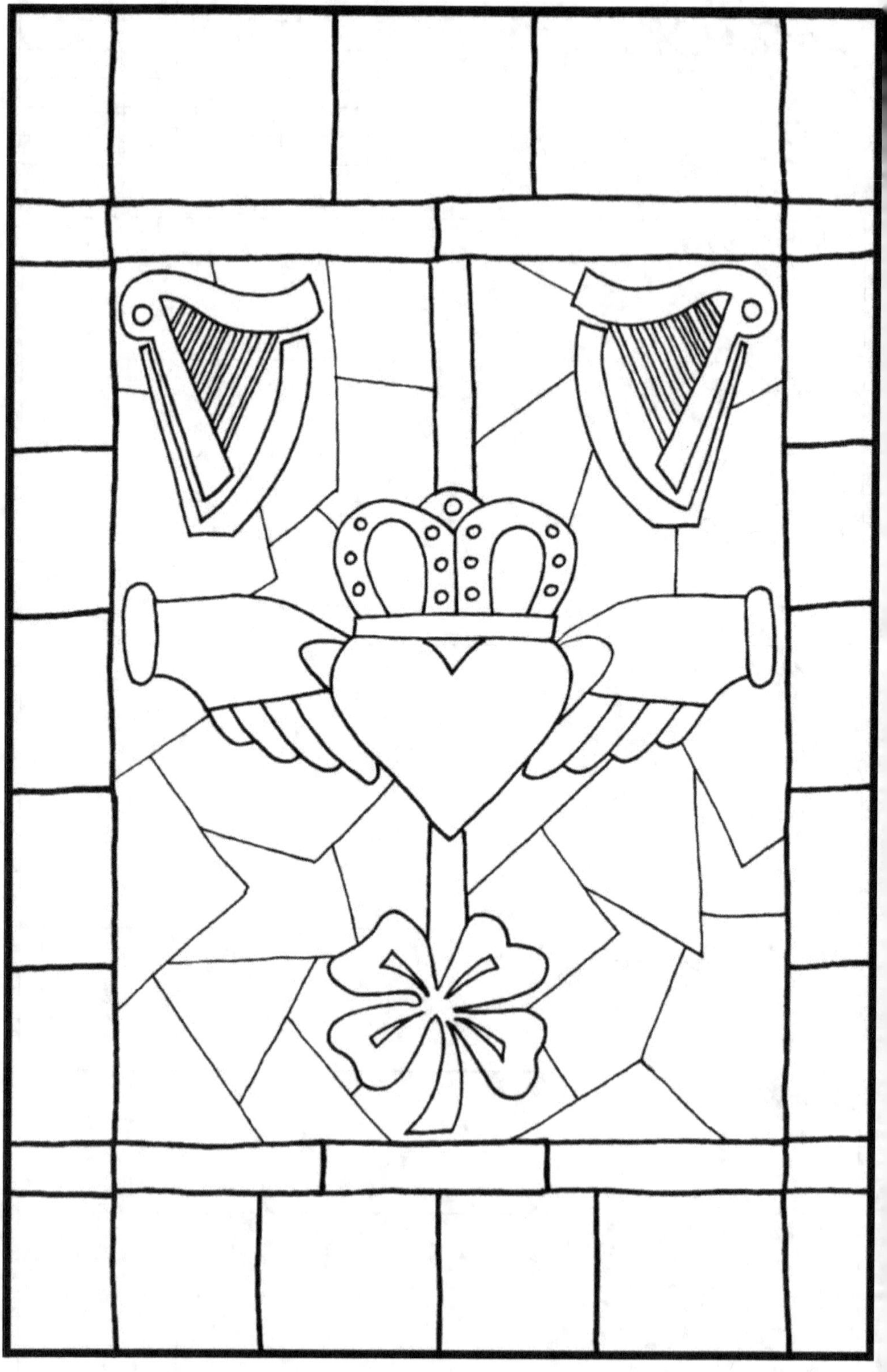

March

WEEK _____

M	T	W	T	F	S	S

Monday

Tuesday

Wednesday

Thursday

Friday

Saturday

Sunday

Notes

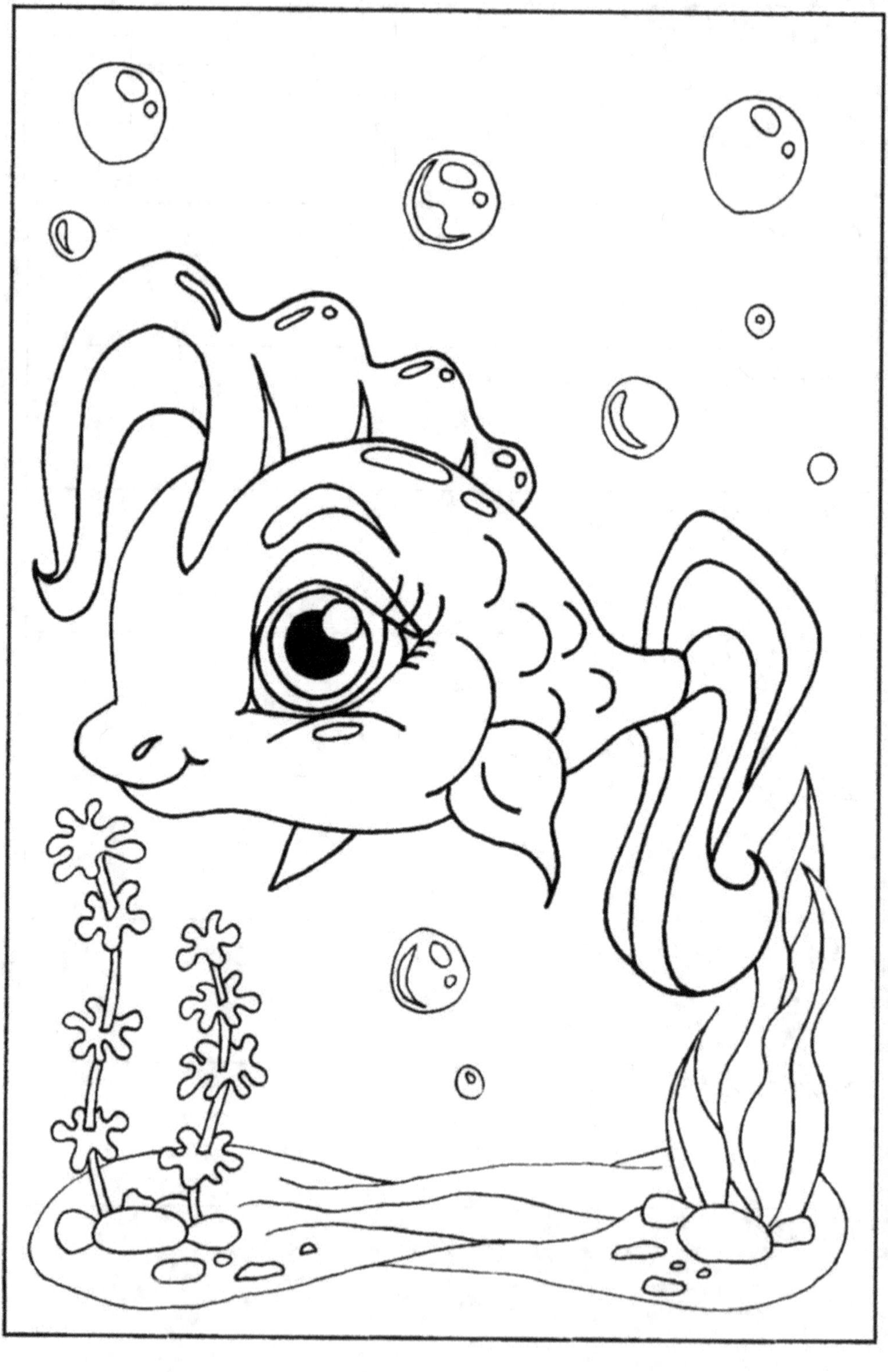

March

WEEK _____

M	T	W	T	F	S	S

Monday

Tuesday

Wednesday

Thursday

Friday

Saturday

Sunday

Notes

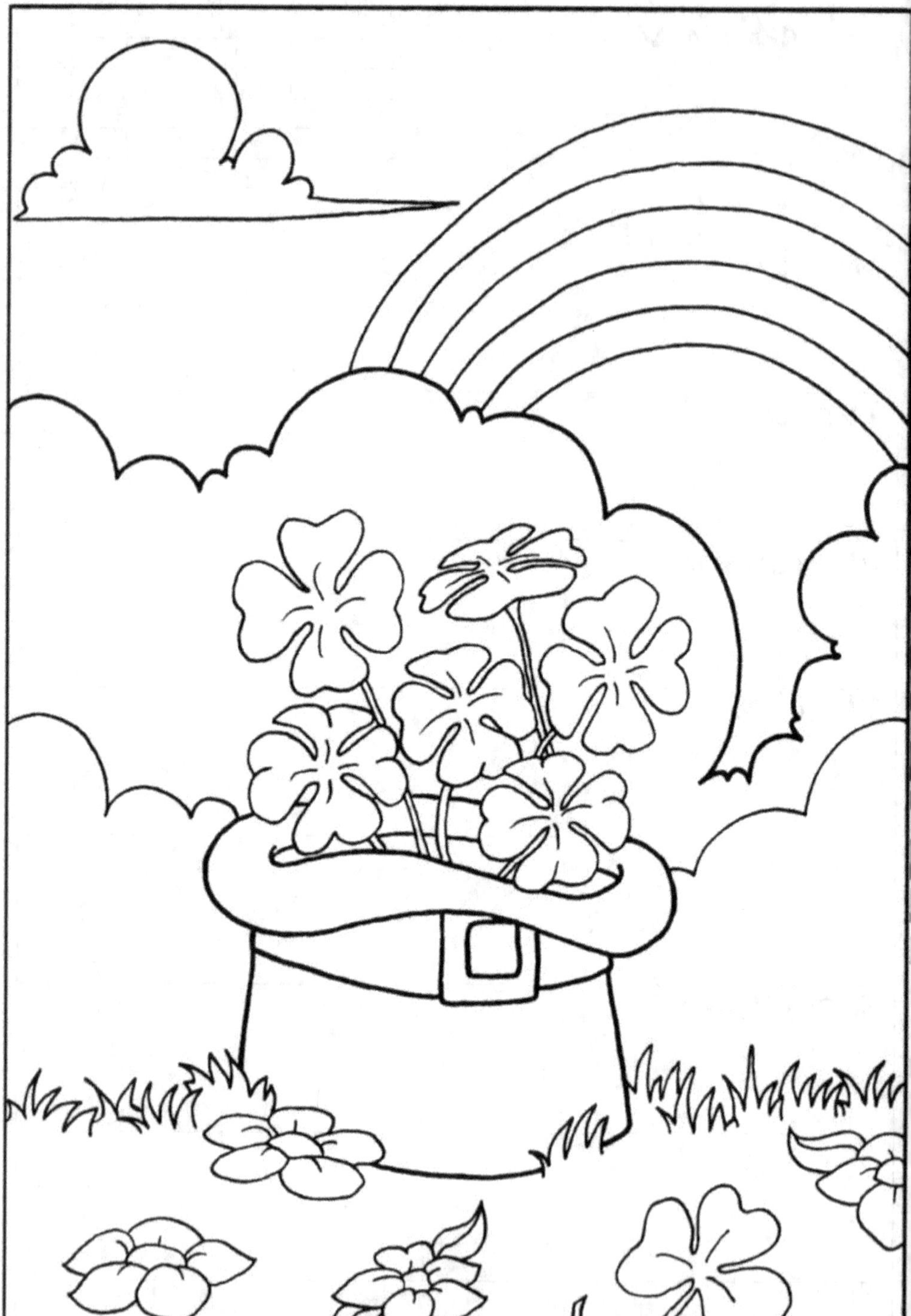

March

WEEK _____

M	T	W	T	F	S	S

Monday

Tuesday

Wednesday

Thursday

Friday

Saturday

Sunday

Notes

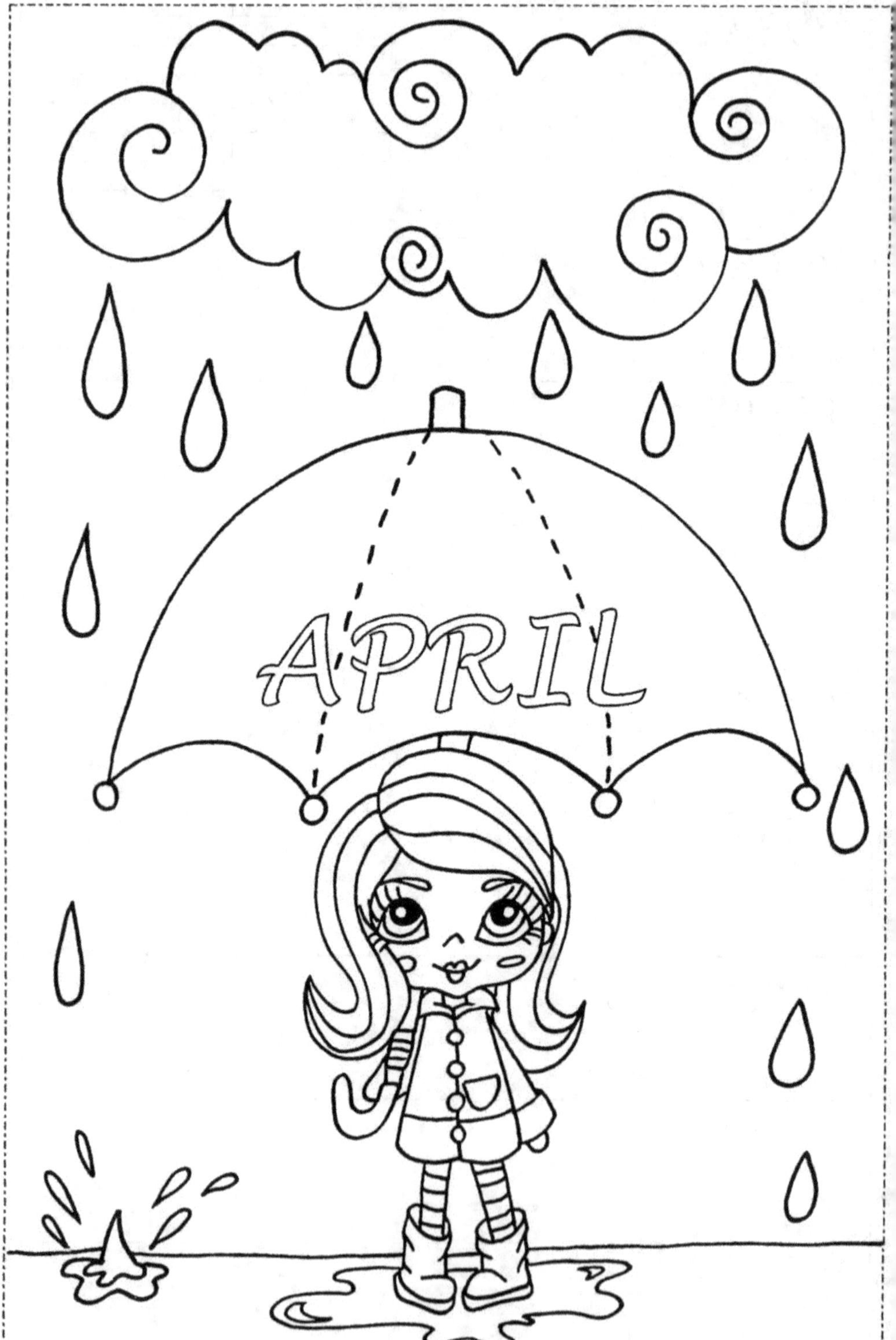
APRIL

Month at a glance ...

April

M	T	W	T	F	S	S

April To Do:

- ○ ________________________________
- ○ ________________________________
- ○ ________________________________
- ○ ________________________________
- ○ ________________________________
- ○ ________________________________
- ○ ________________________________
- ○ ________________________________
- ○ ________________________________

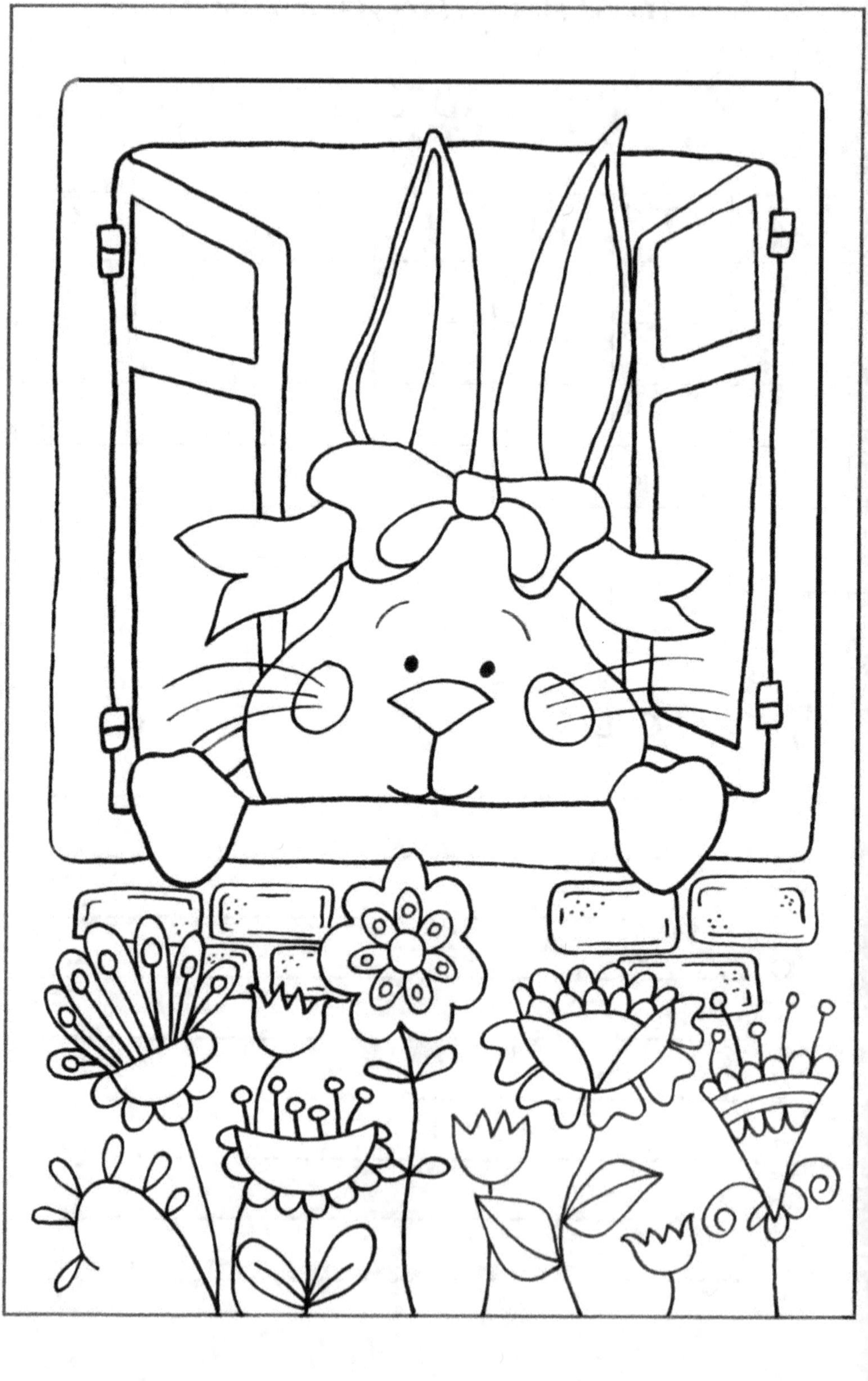

April

WEEK _____

M	T	W	T	F	S	S

Monday

Tuesday

Wednesday

Thursday

Friday

Saturday

Sunday

Notes

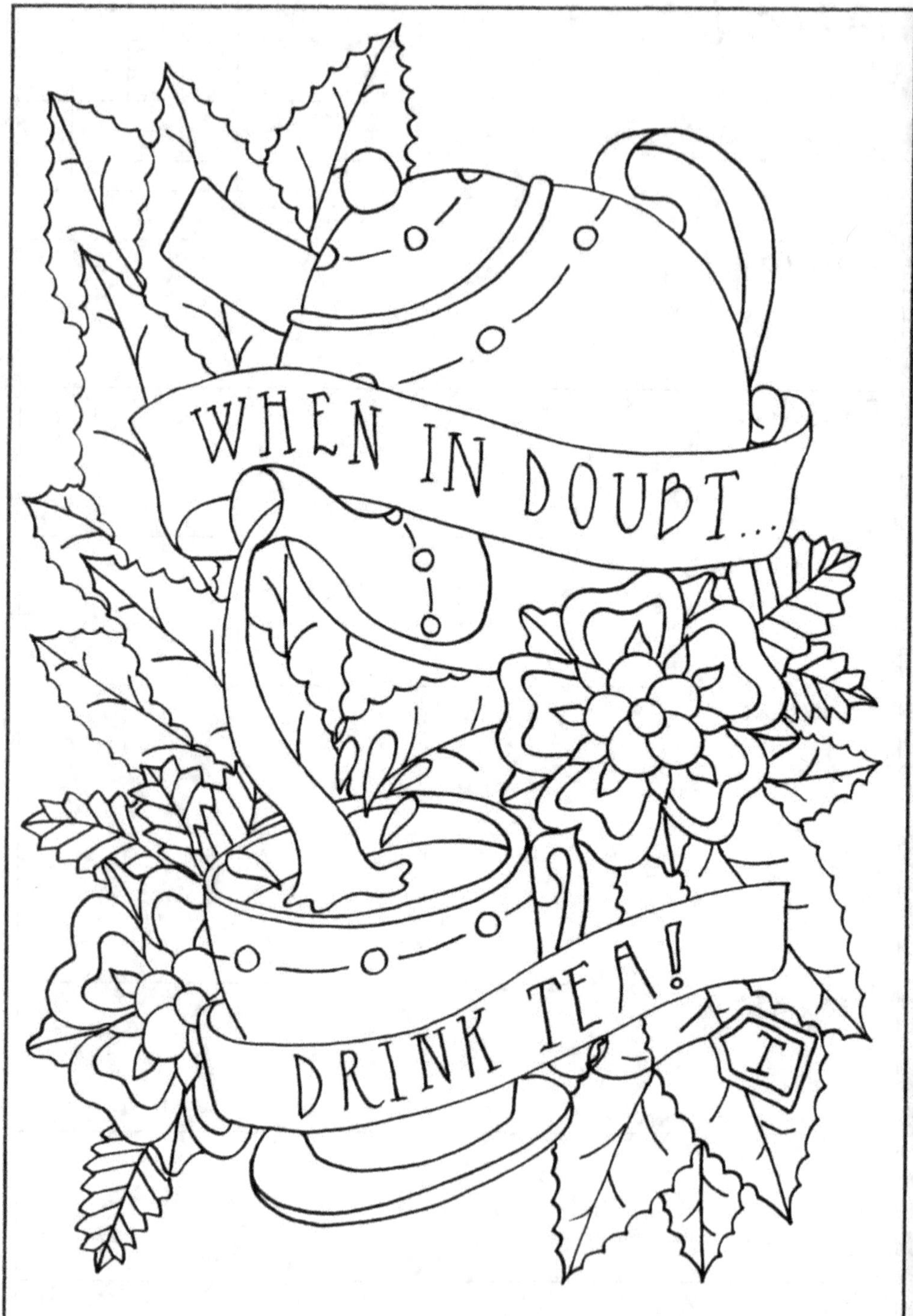
WHEN IN DOUBT...
DRINK TEA!
T

April

WEEK _____

M	T	W	T	F	S	S

Monday

Tuesday

Wednesday

Thursday

Friday

Saturday

Sunday

Notes

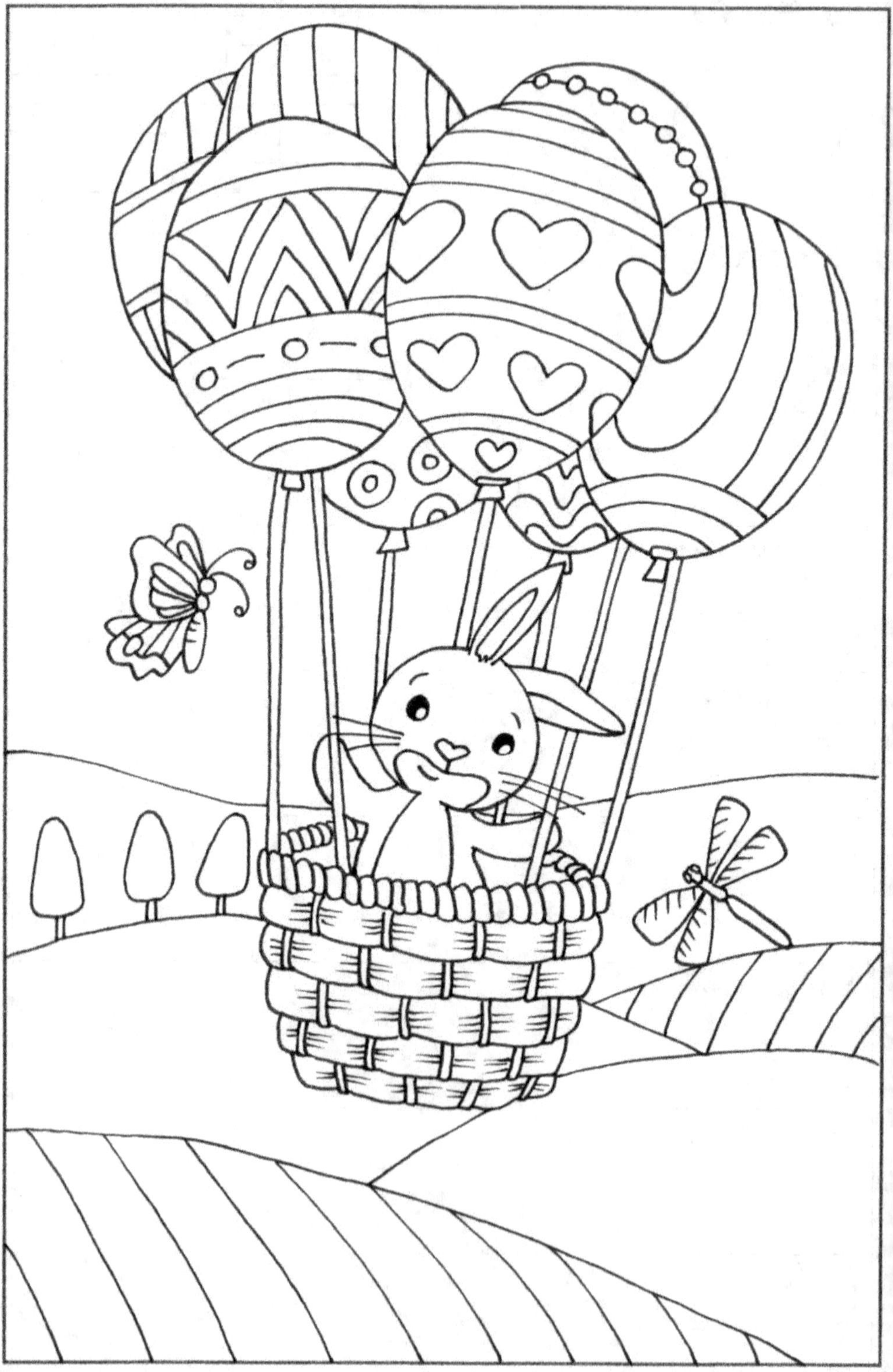

April

WEEK _____

M	T	W	T	F	S	S

Monday

Tuesday

Wednesday

Thursday

Friday

Saturday

Sunday

Notes

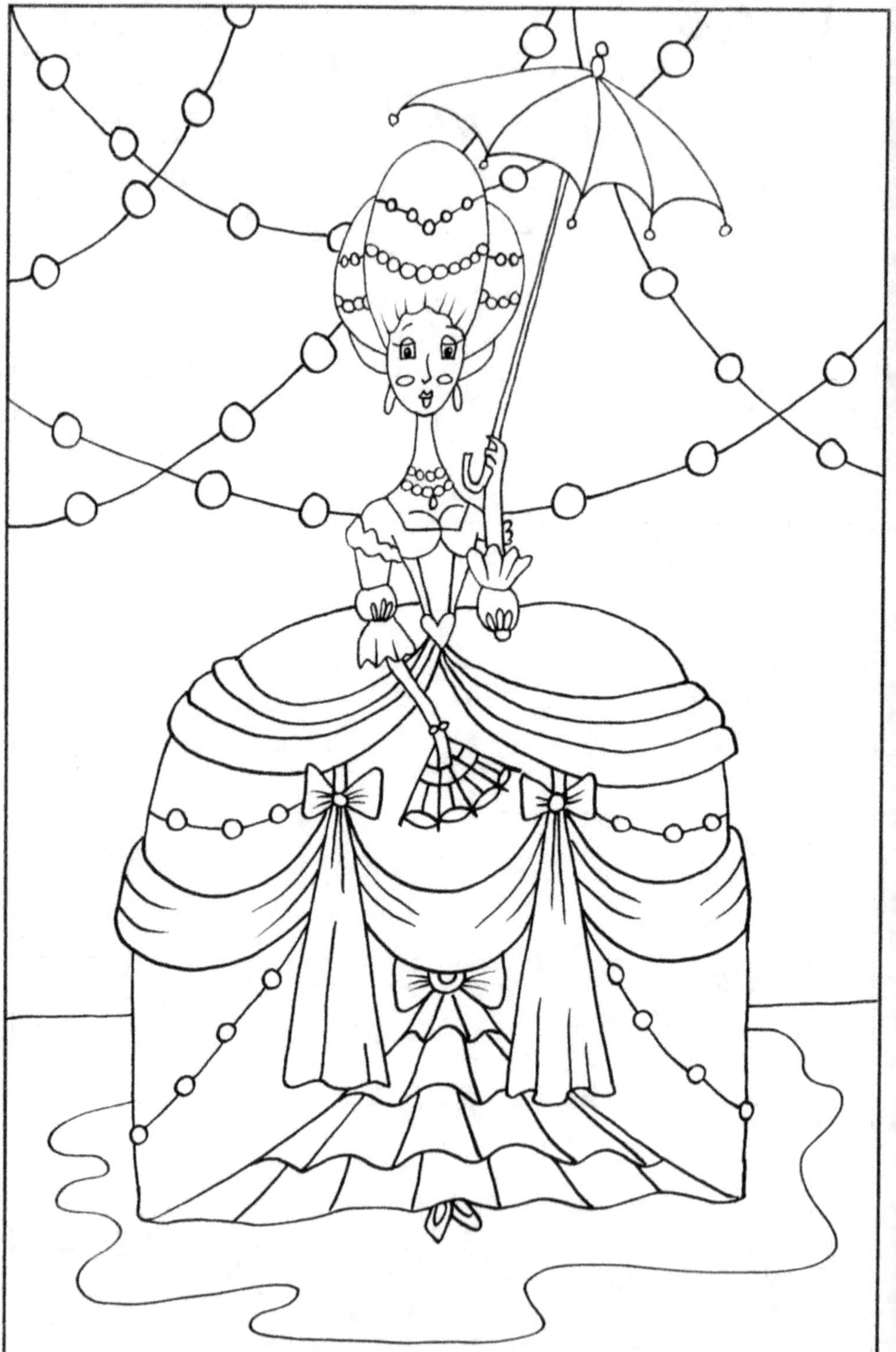

April

WEEK _____

M	T	W	T	F	S	S

Monday

Tuesday

Wednesday

Thursday

Friday

Saturday

Sunday

Notes

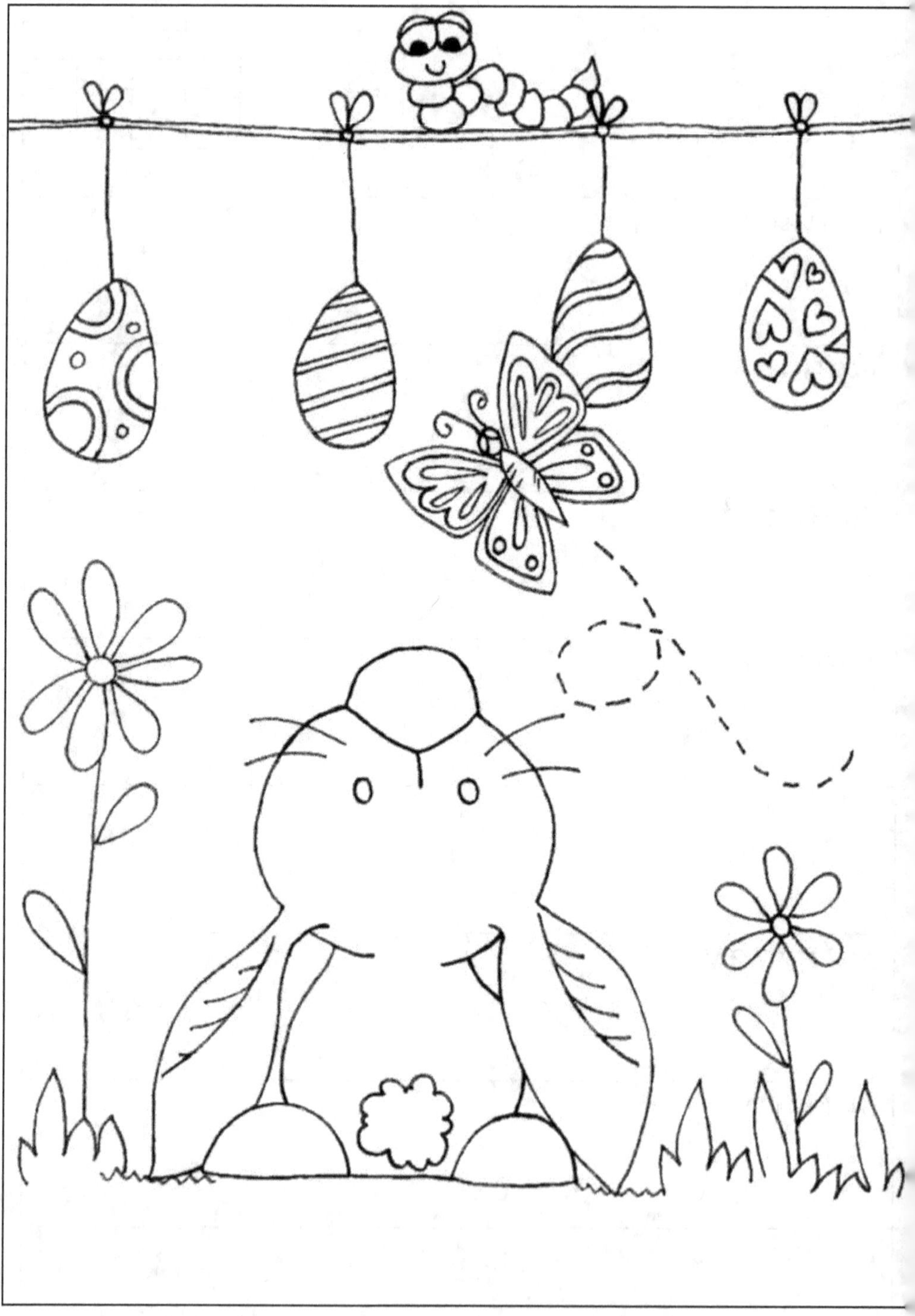

April

WEEK _____

M	T	W	T	F	S	S

Monday

Tuesday

Wednesday

Thursday

Friday

Saturday

Sunday

Notes

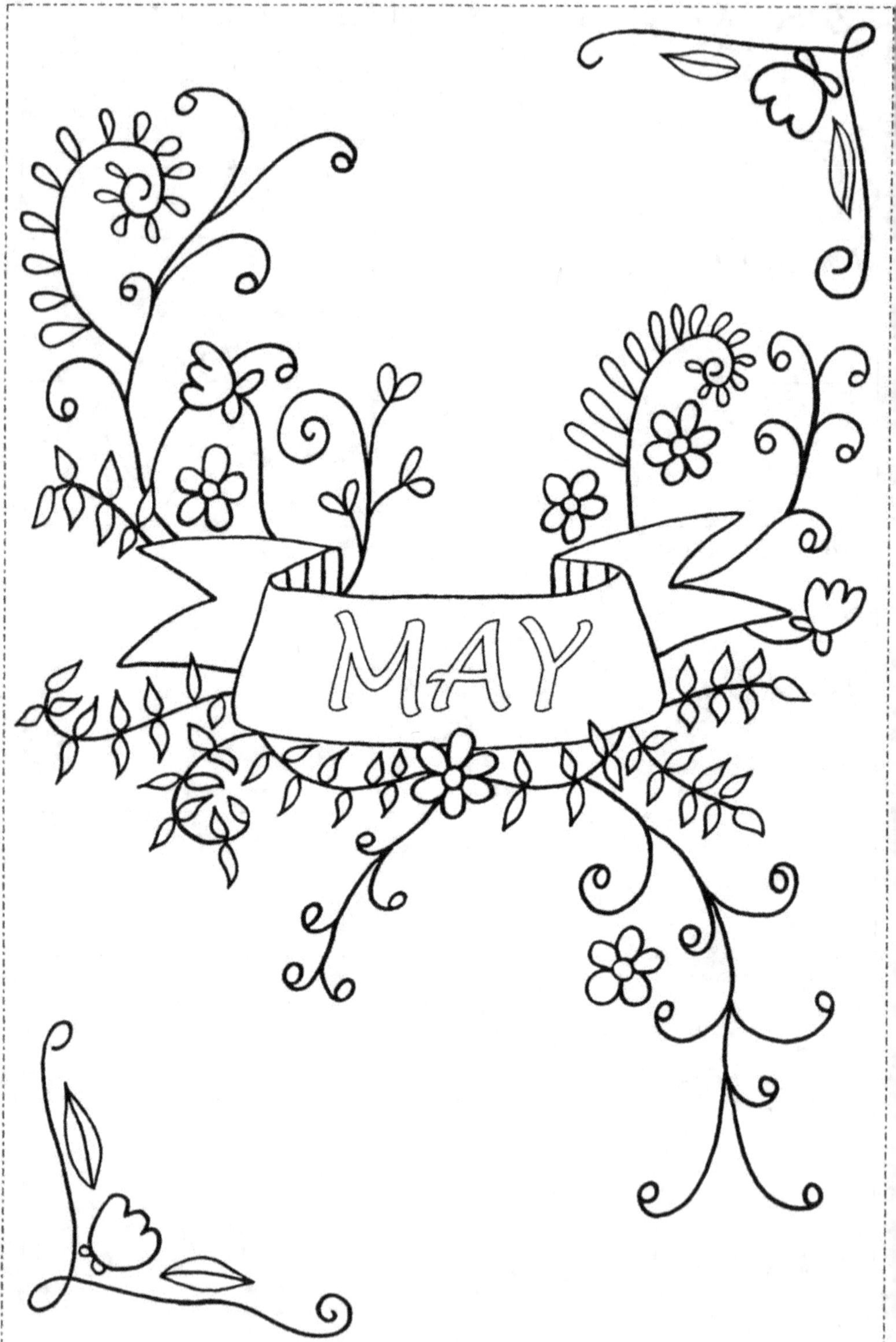
MAY

Month at a glance…

May

M	T	W	T	F	S	S

May To Do:

- ○ ________________________________
- ○ ________________________________
- ○ ________________________________
- ○ ________________________________
- ○ ________________________________
- ○ ________________________________
- ○ ________________________________
- ○ ________________________________
- ○ ________________________________
- ○ ________________________________

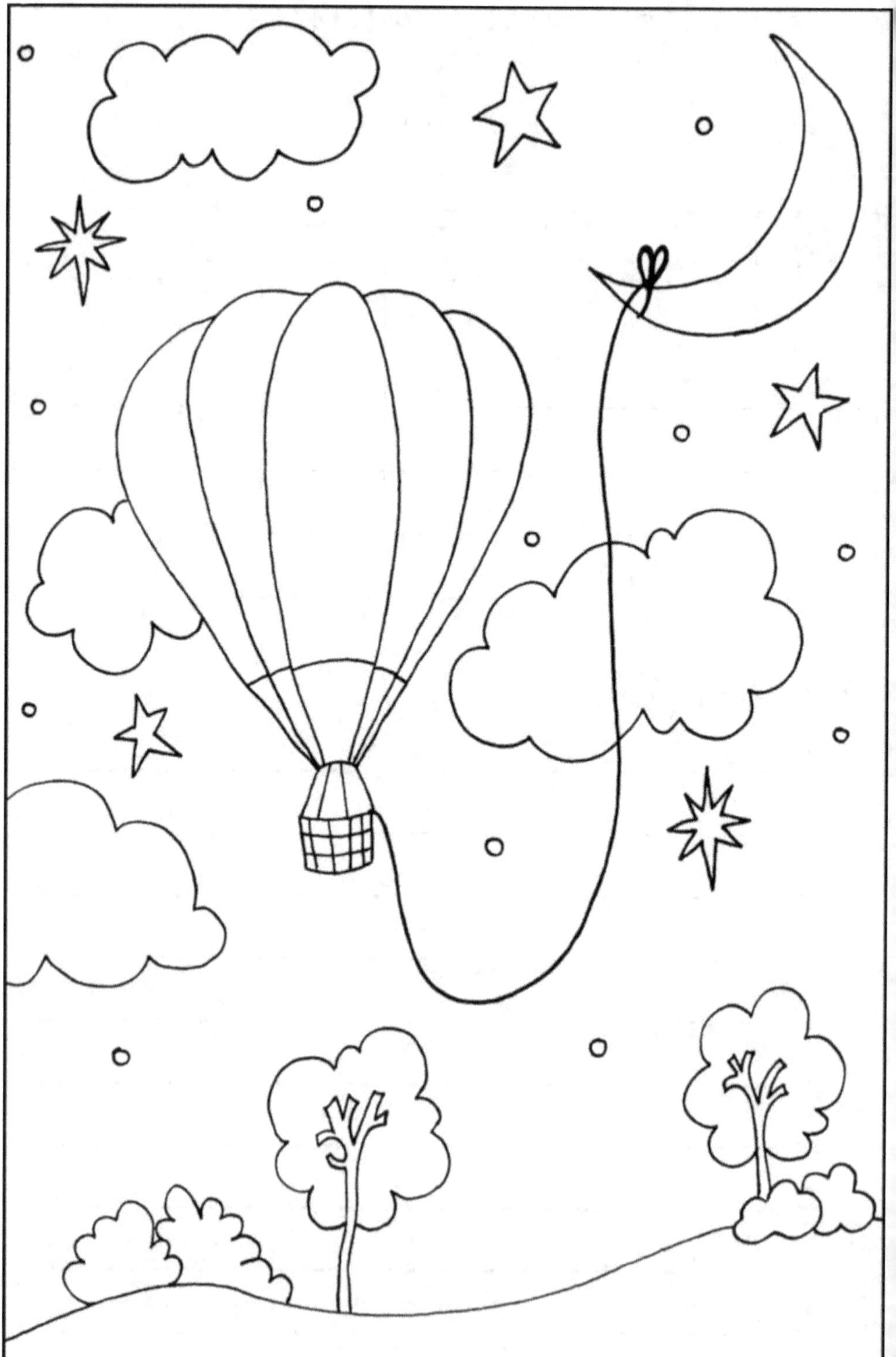

May

WEEK _____

M	T	W	T	F	S	S

Monday

Tuesday

Wednesday

Thursday

Friday

Saturday

Sunday

Notes

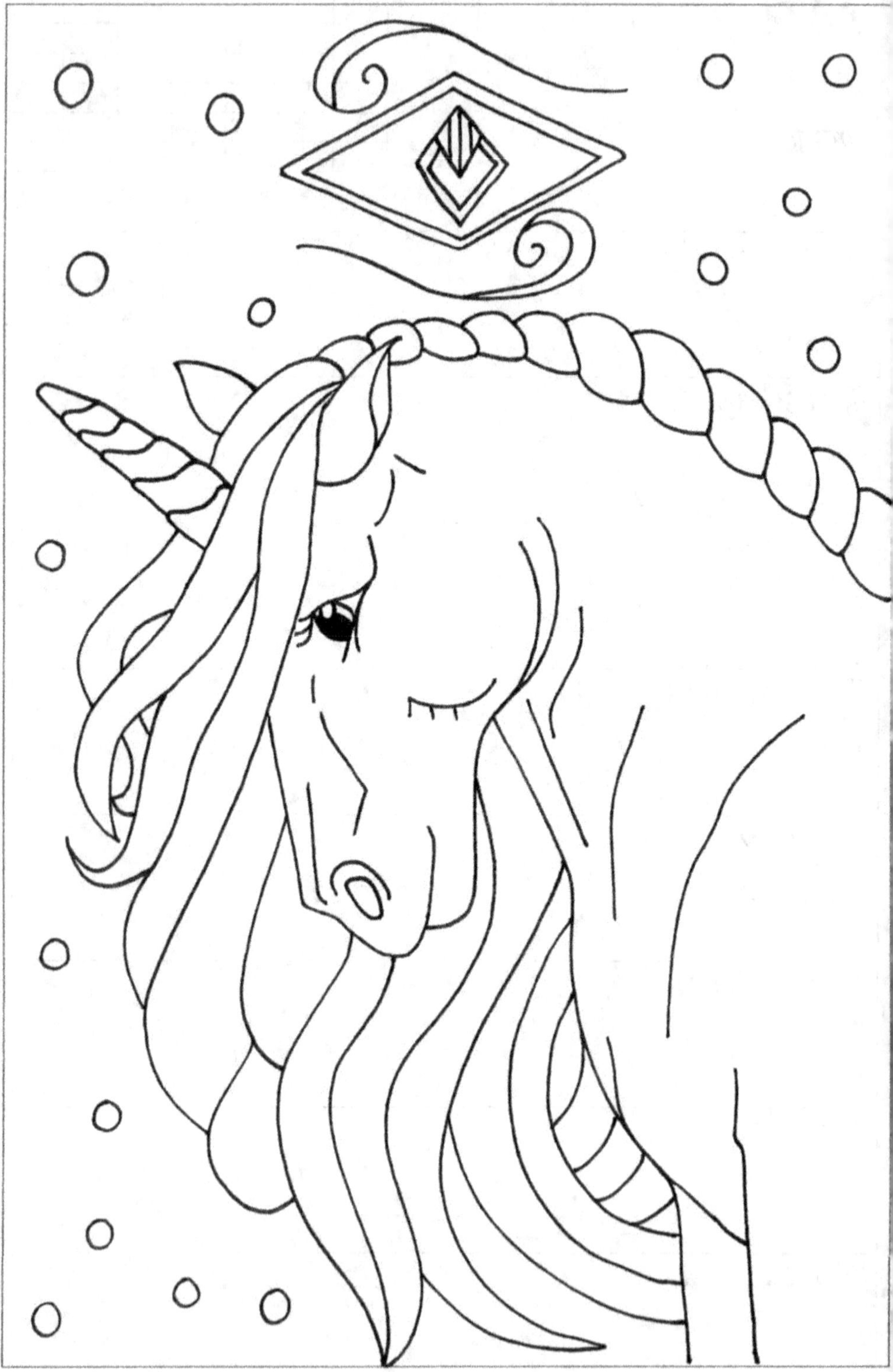

May

WEEK _____

M	T	W	T	F	S	S

Monday

Tuesday

Wednesday

Thursday

Friday

Saturday

Sunday

Notes

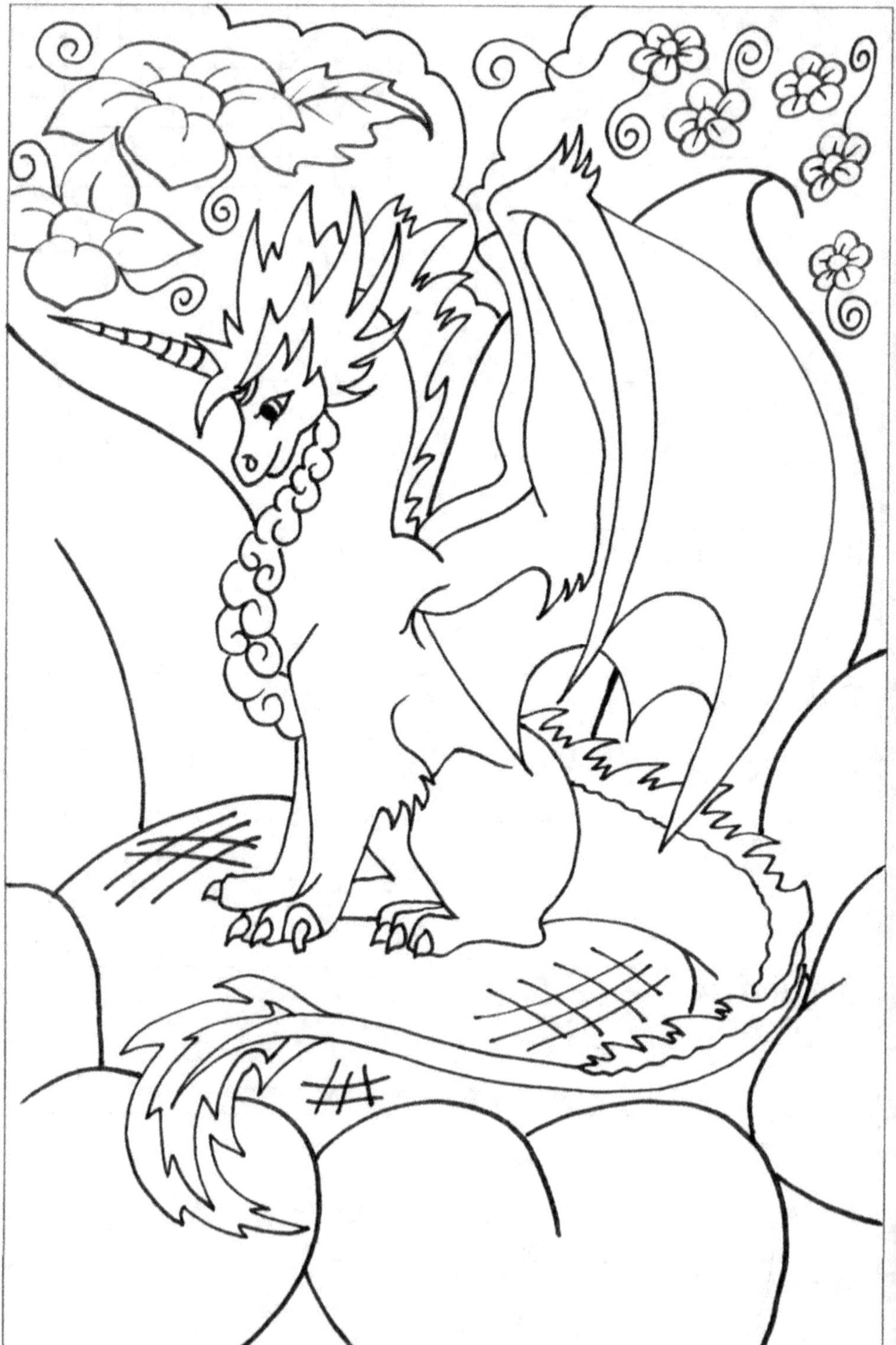

May

WEEK _____

M	T	W	T	F	S	S

Monday

Tuesday

Wednesday

Thursday

Friday

Saturday

Sunday

Notes

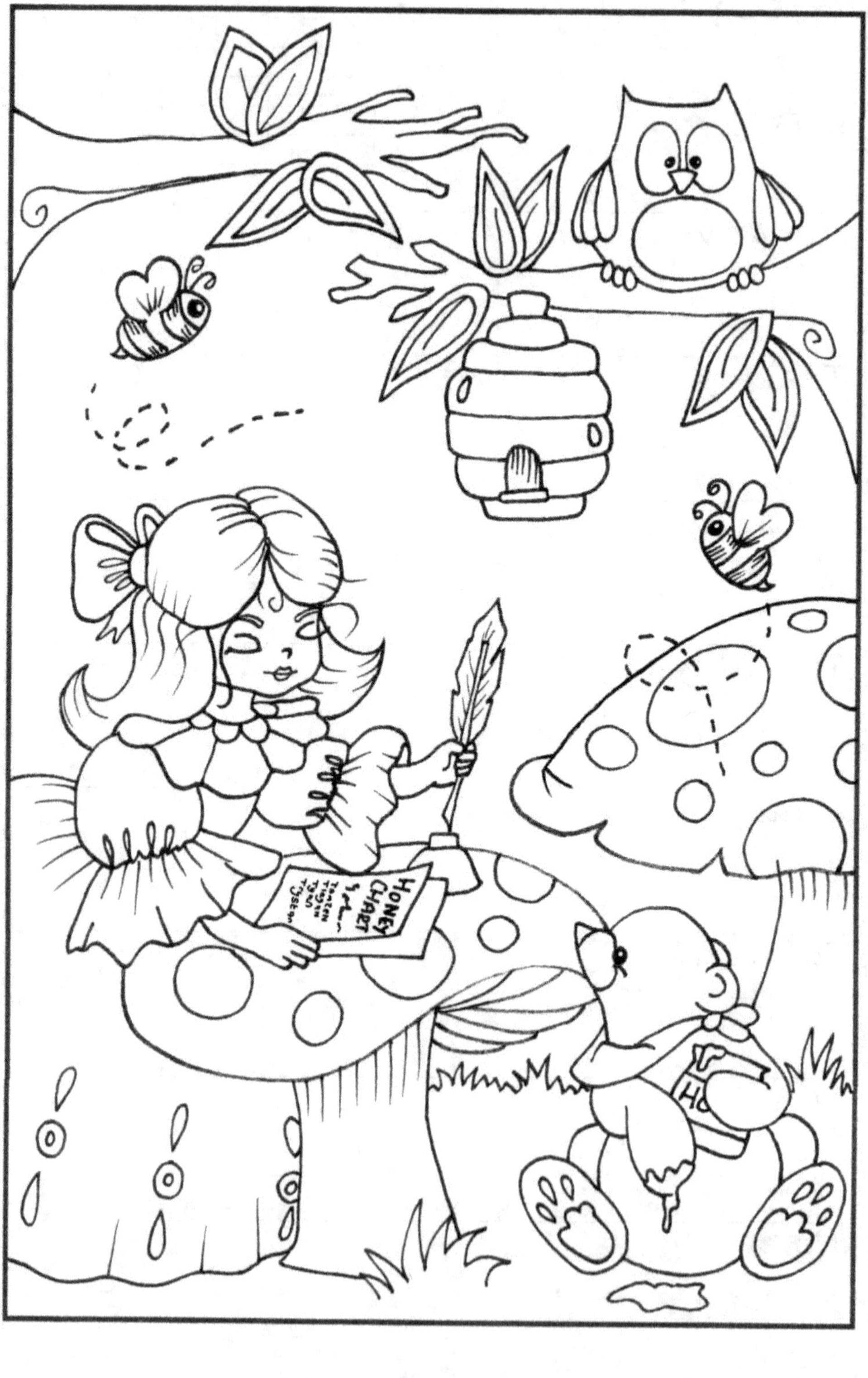
HONEY CHART

May

WEEK _____

M	T	W	T	F	S	S

Monday

Tuesday

Wednesday

Thursday

Friday

Saturday

Sunday

Notes

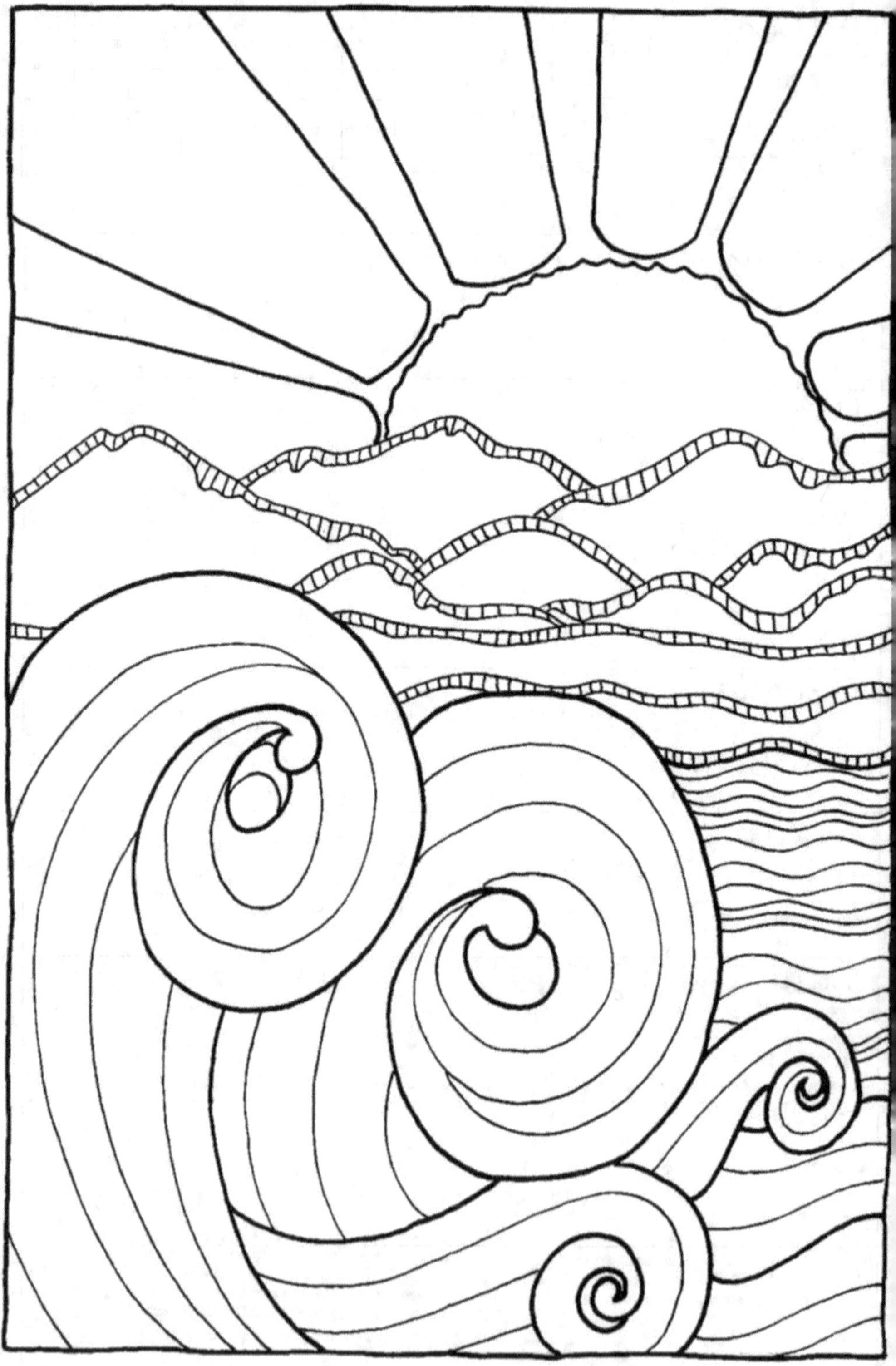

May

WEEK _____

M	T	W	T	F	S	S

Monday
Tuesday
Wednesday
Thursday
Friday
Saturday
Sunday
Notes

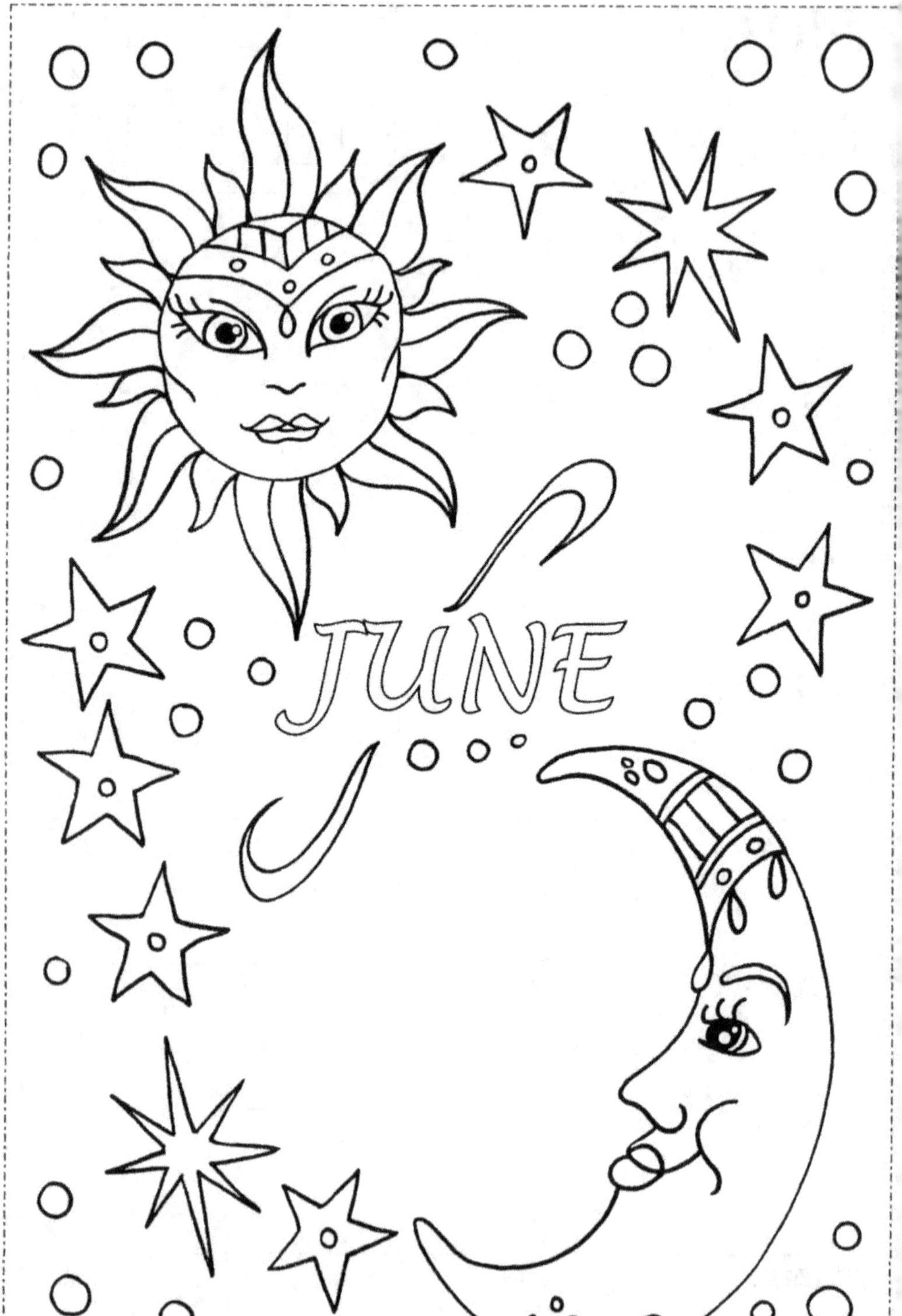
JUNE

Month at a glance...

June

M	T	W	T	F	S	S

June To Do:

- ○ ______________________________
- ○ ______________________________
- ○ ______________________________
- ○ ______________________________
- ○ ______________________________
- ○ ______________________________
- ○ ______________________________
- ○ ______________________________
- ○ ______________________________
- ○ ______________________________

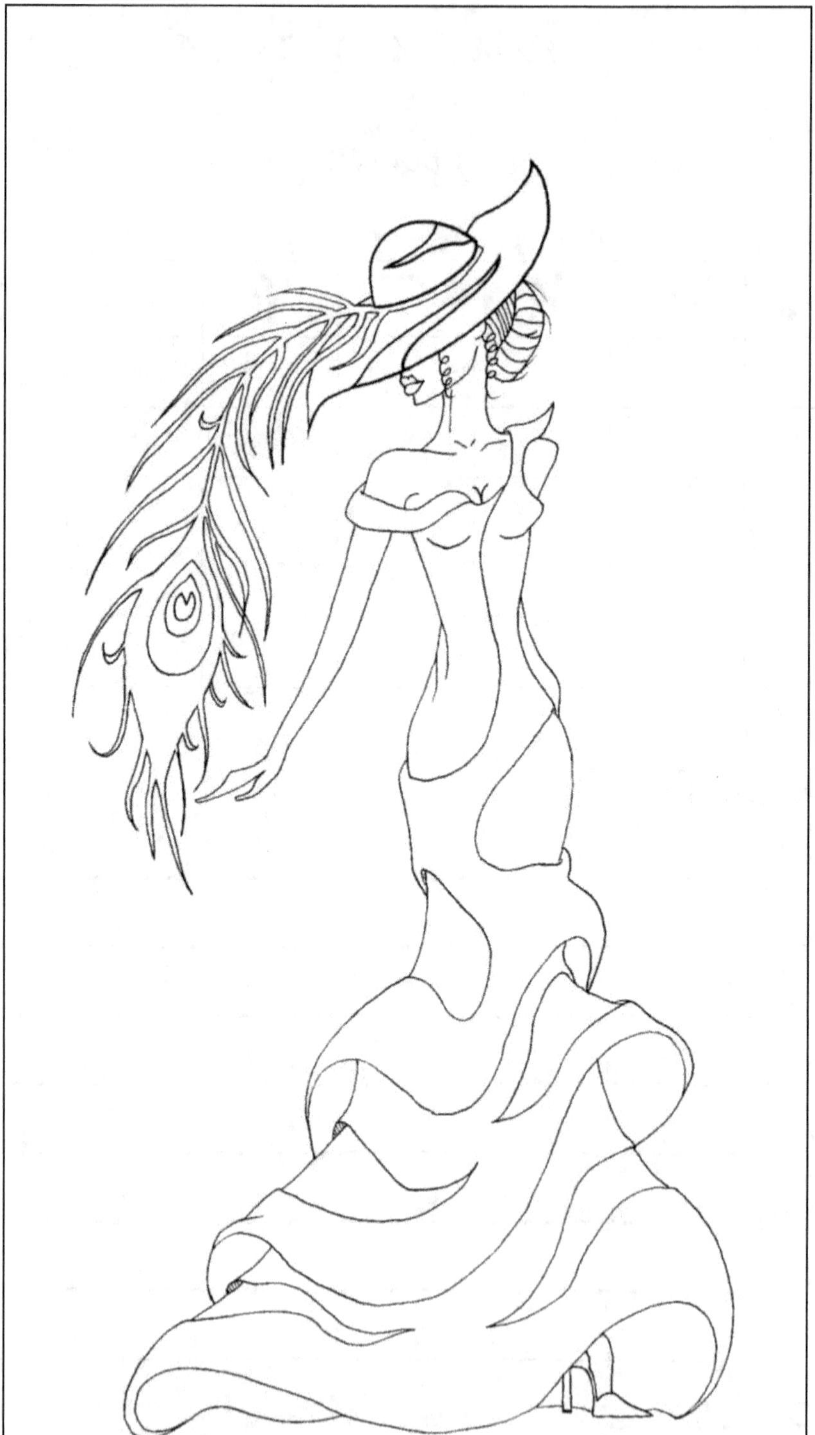

June

WEEK _____

M	T	W	T	F	S	S

Monday

Tuesday

Wednesday

Thursday

Friday

Saturday

Sunday

Notes

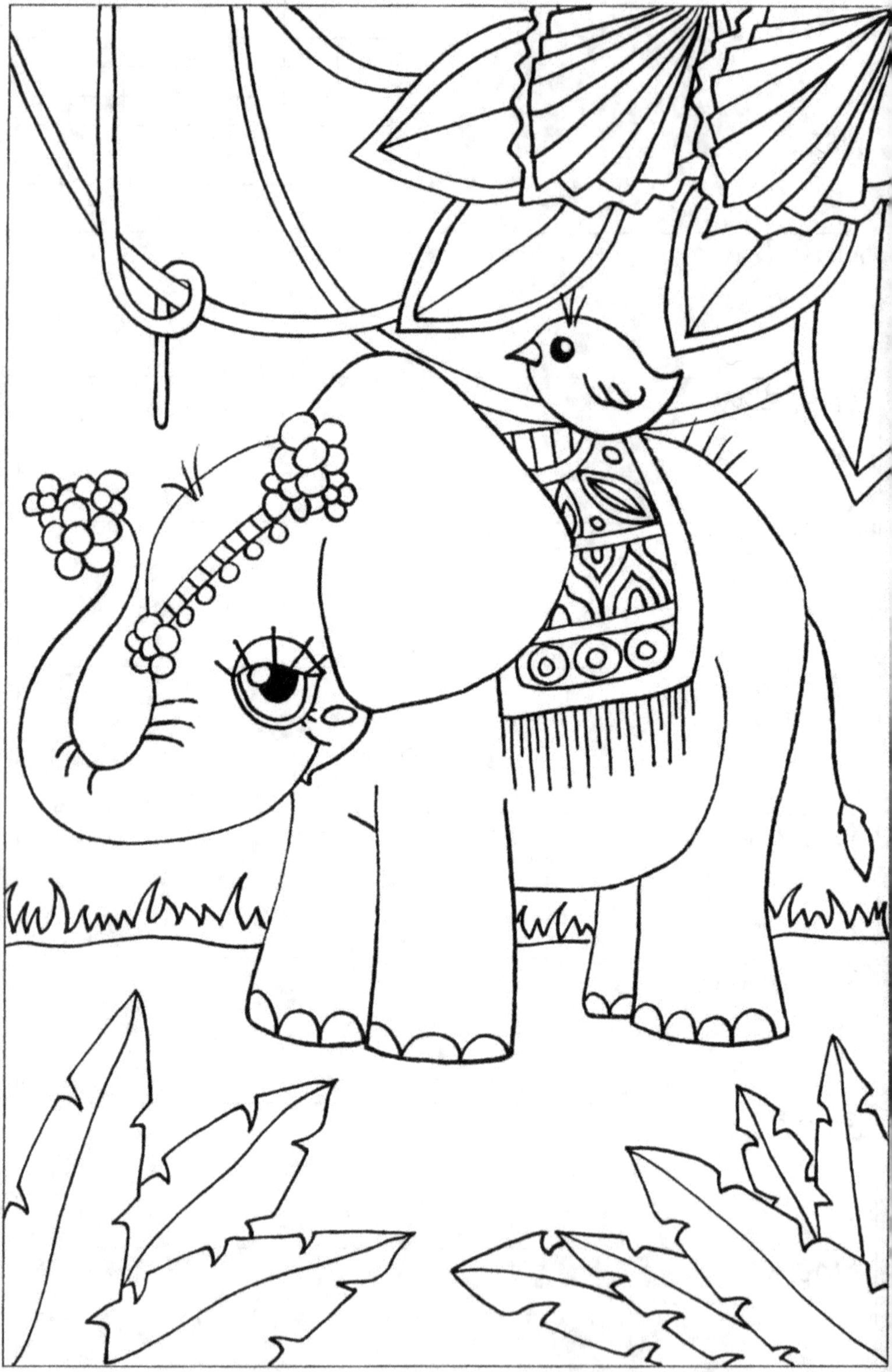

June

WEEK _____

M	T	W	T	F	S	S

Monday

Tuesday

Wednesday

Thursday

Friday

Saturday

Sunday

Notes

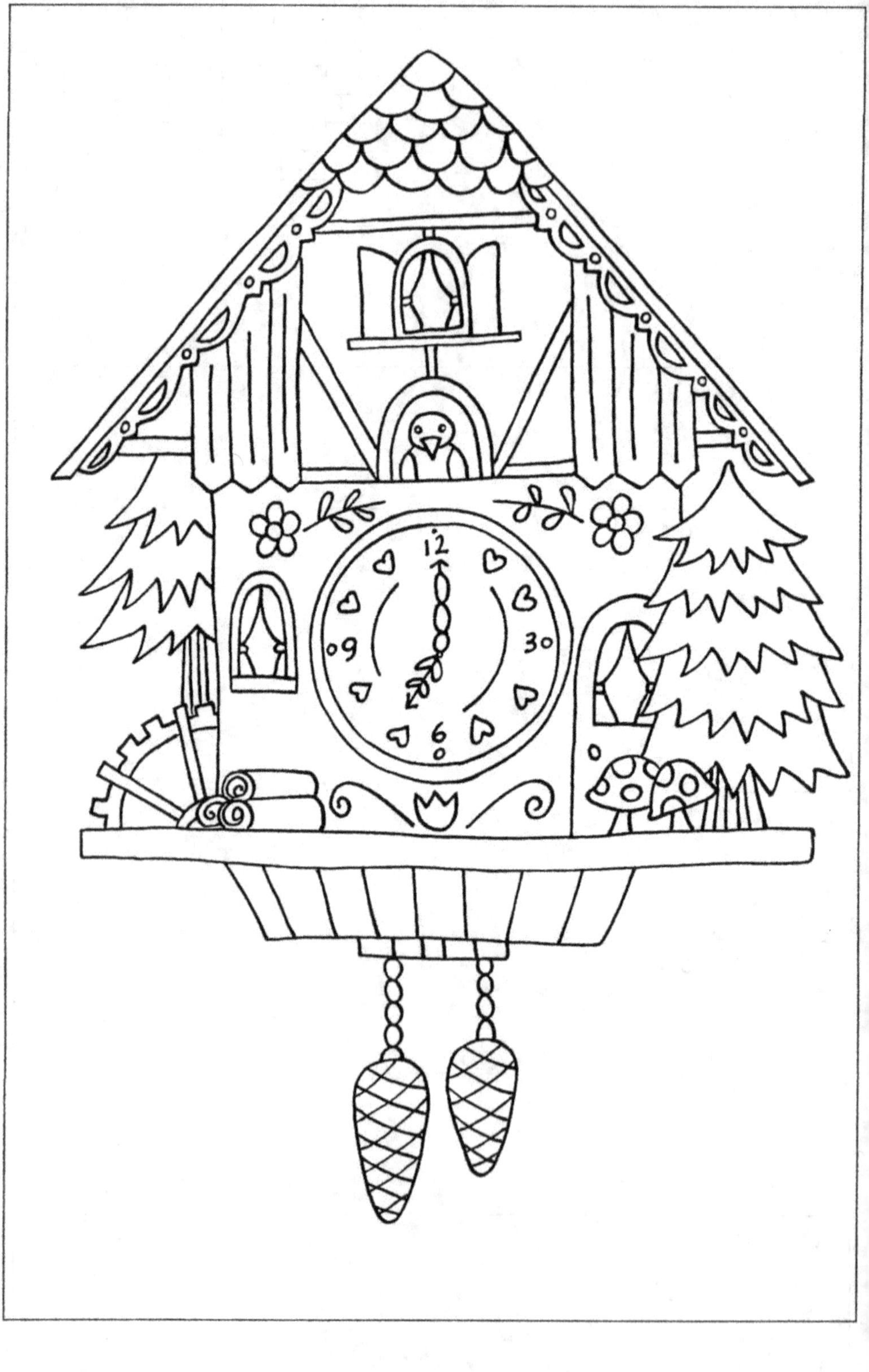
12
9
3
6

June

WEEK _____

M	T	W	T	F	S	S

Monday

Tuesday

Wednesday

Thursday

Friday

Saturday

Sunday

Notes

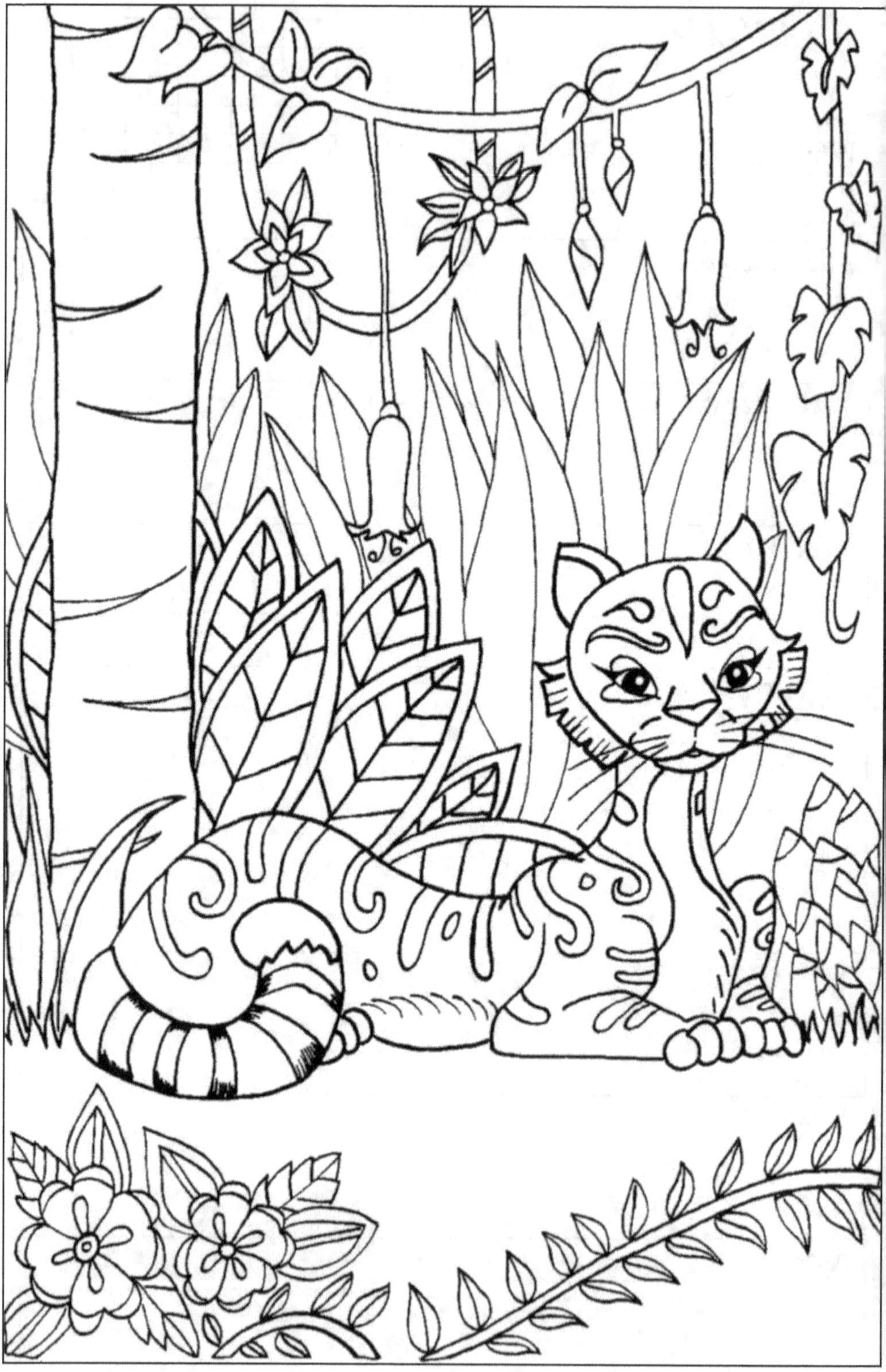

June

WEEK _____

M	T	W	T	F	S	S

Monday

Tuesday

Wednesday

Thursday

Friday

Saturday

Sunday

Notes

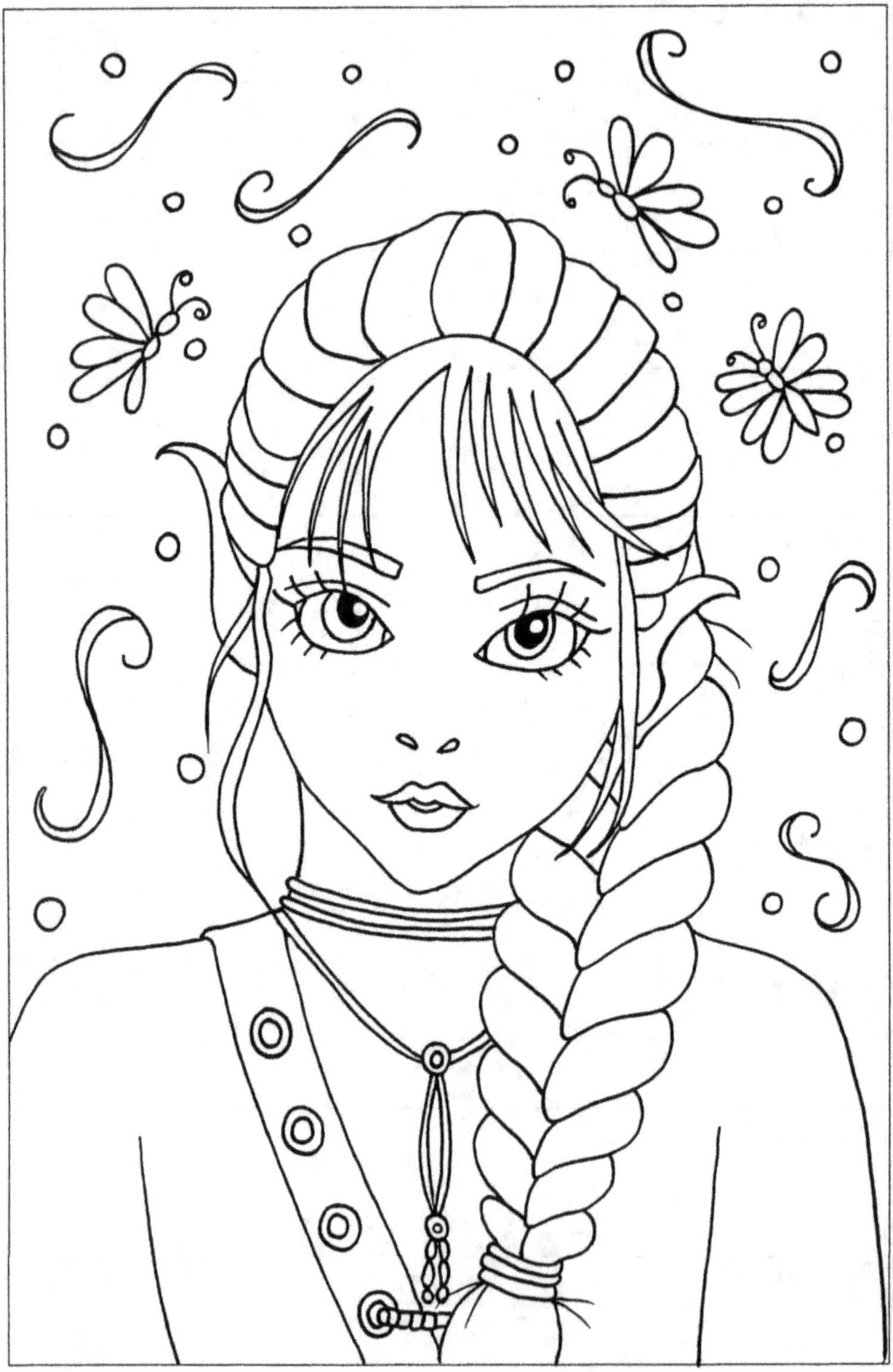

June

WEEK _____

M	T	W	T	F	S	S

Monday

Tuesday

Wednesday

Thursday

Friday

Saturday

Sunday

Notes

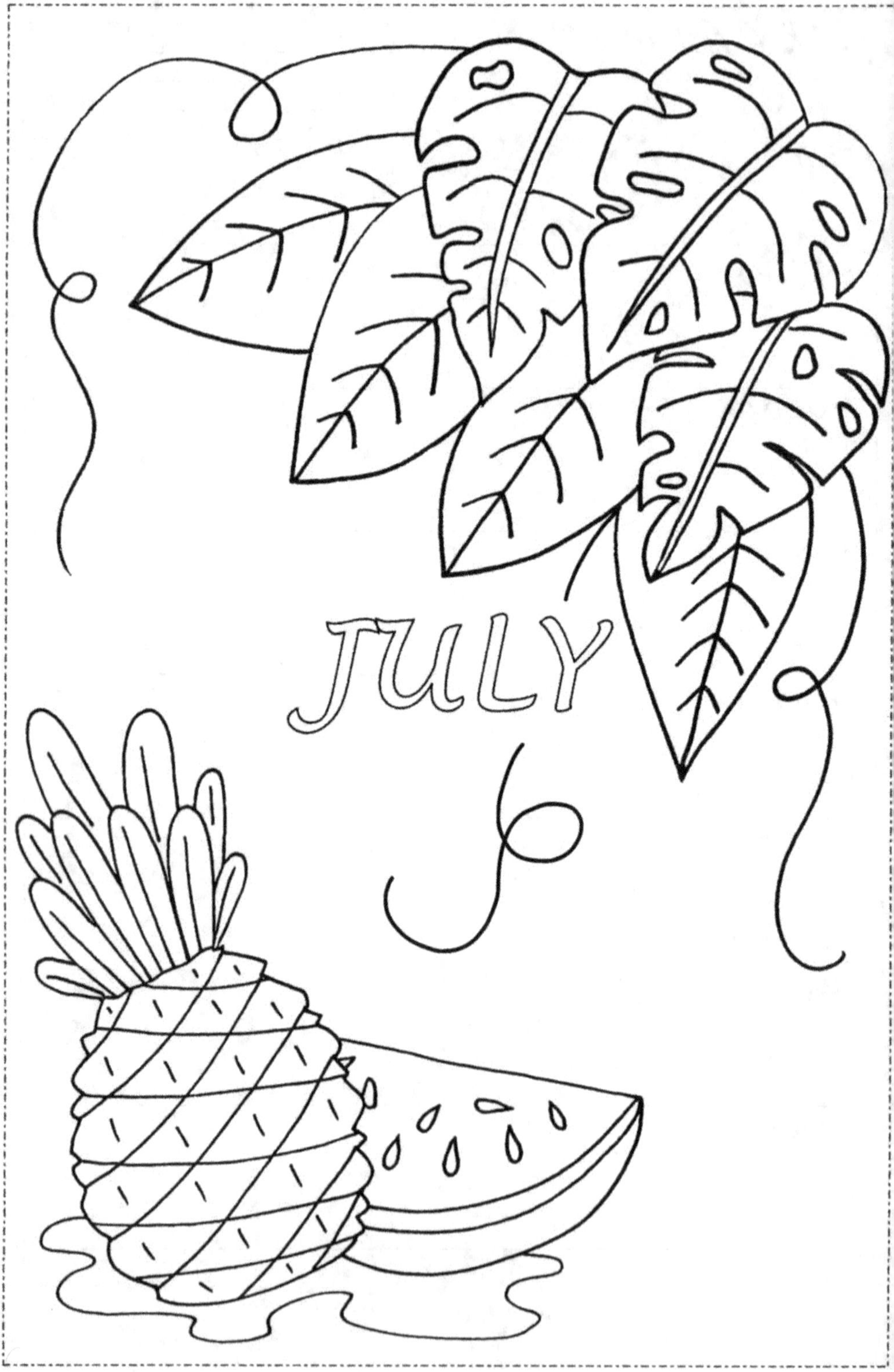
JULY

Month at a glance …

July

M	T	W	T	F	S	S

July To Do:

- ○ ______________________________
- ○ ______________________________
- ○ ______________________________
- ○ ______________________________
- ○ ______________________________
- ○ ______________________________
- ○ ______________________________
- ○ ______________________________
- ○ ______________________________

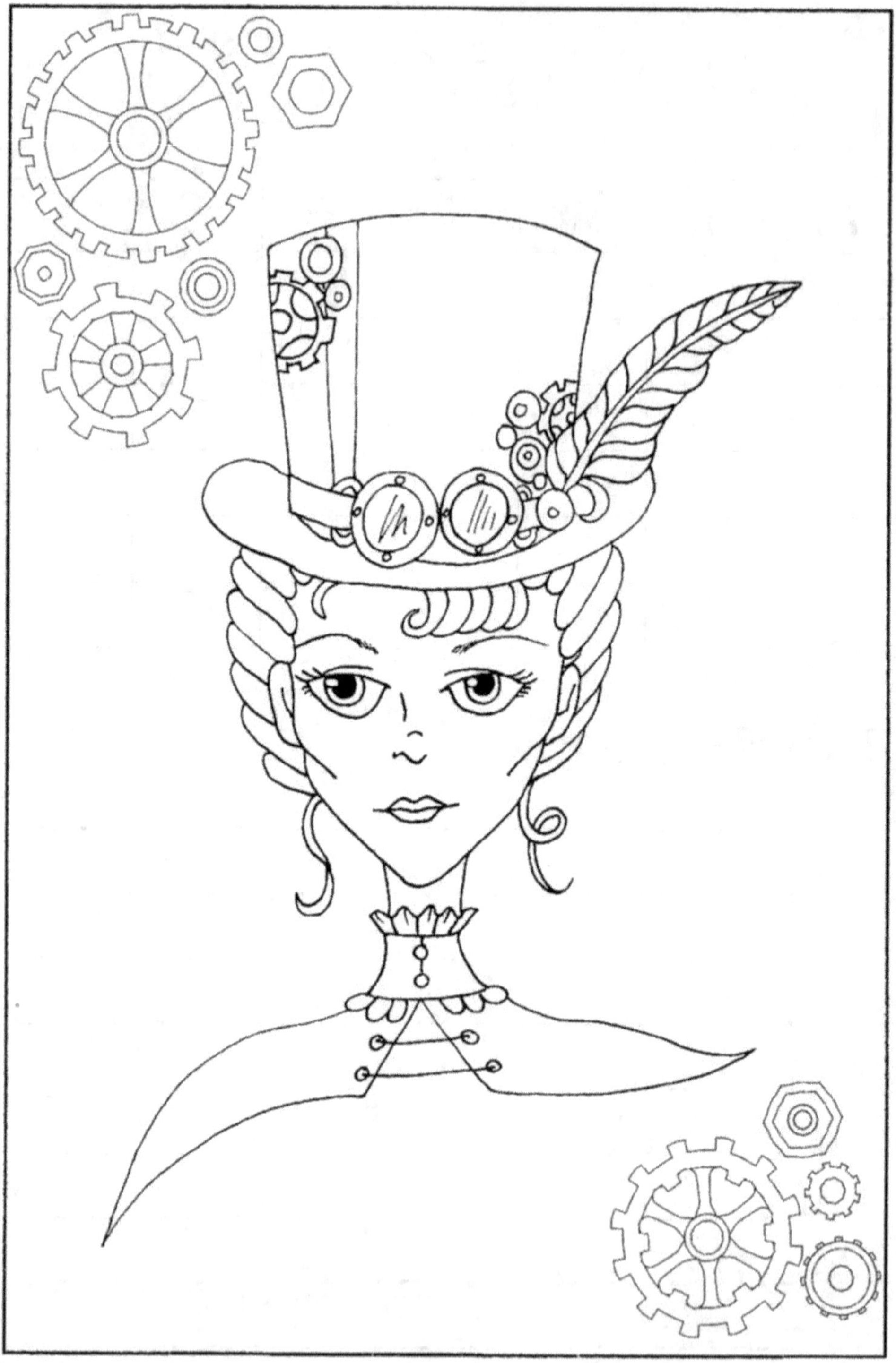

July

WEEK _____

M	T	W	T	F	S	S

Monday
Tuesday
Wednesday
Thursday
Friday
Saturday
Sunday
Notes

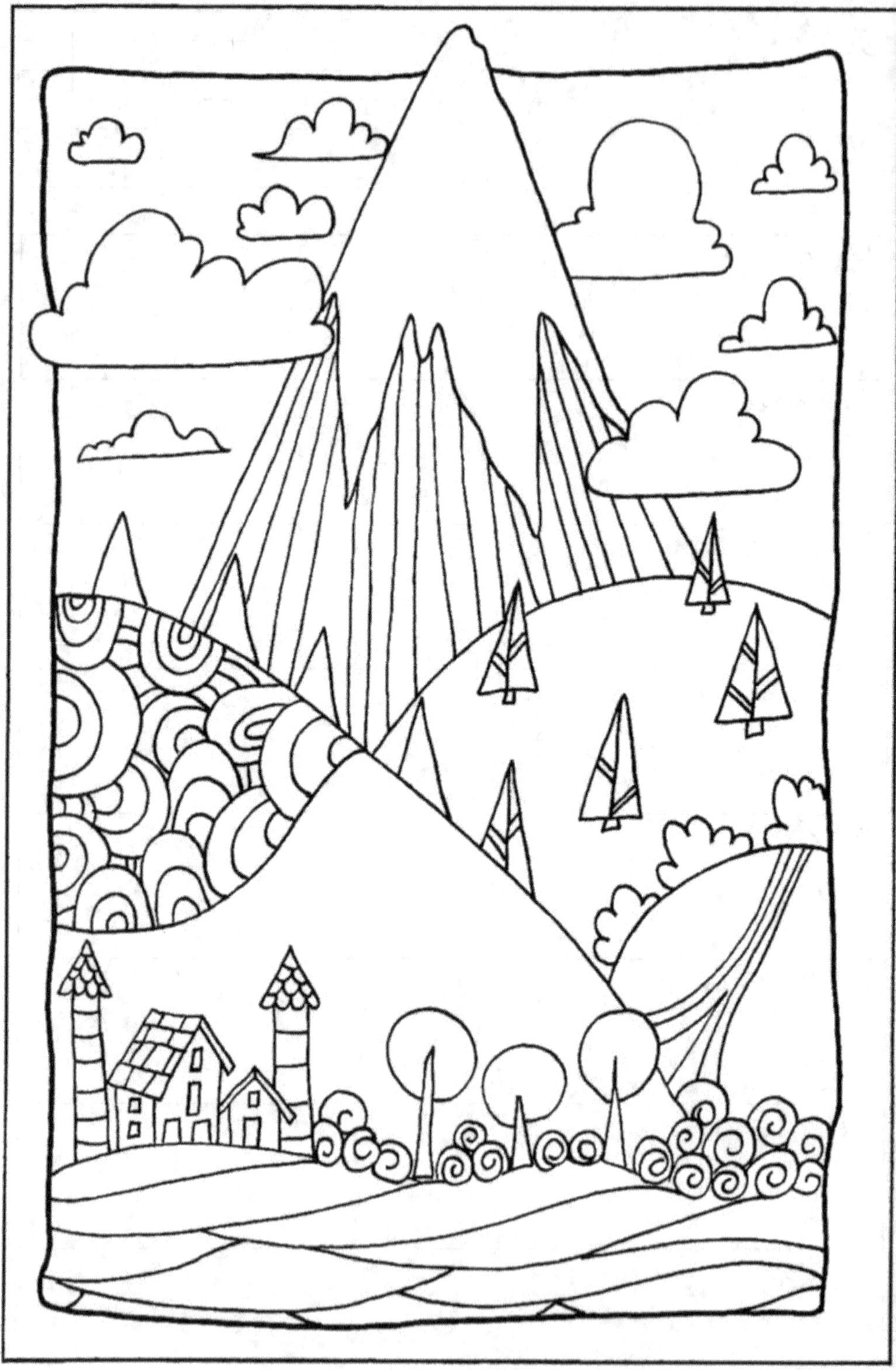

July

WEEK _____

M	T	W	T	F	S	S

Monday

Tuesday

Wednesday

Thursday

Friday

Saturday

Sunday

Notes

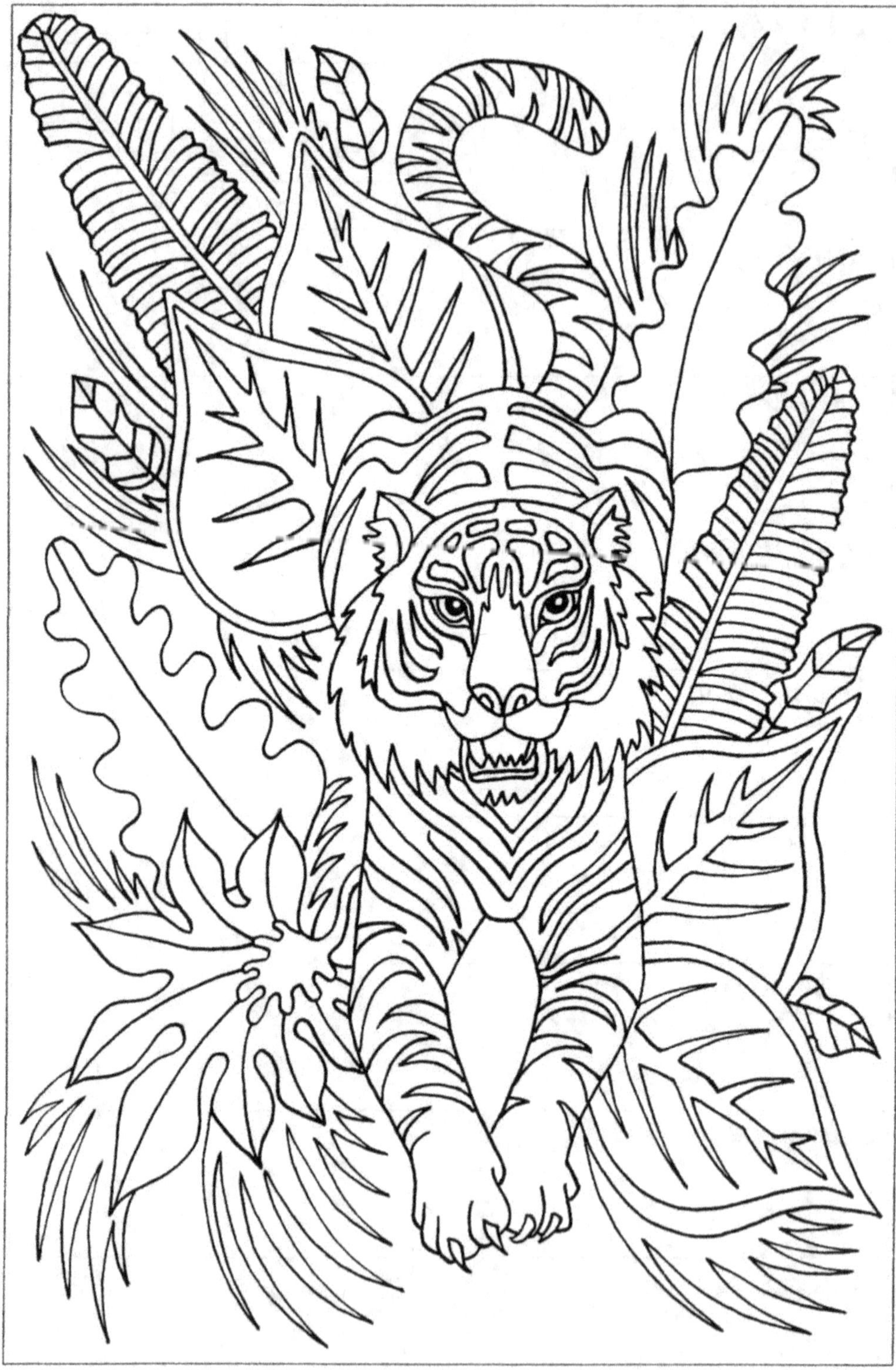

July

WEEK _____

M	T	W	T	F	S	S

Monday

Tuesday

Wednesday

Thursday

Friday

Saturday

Sunday

Notes

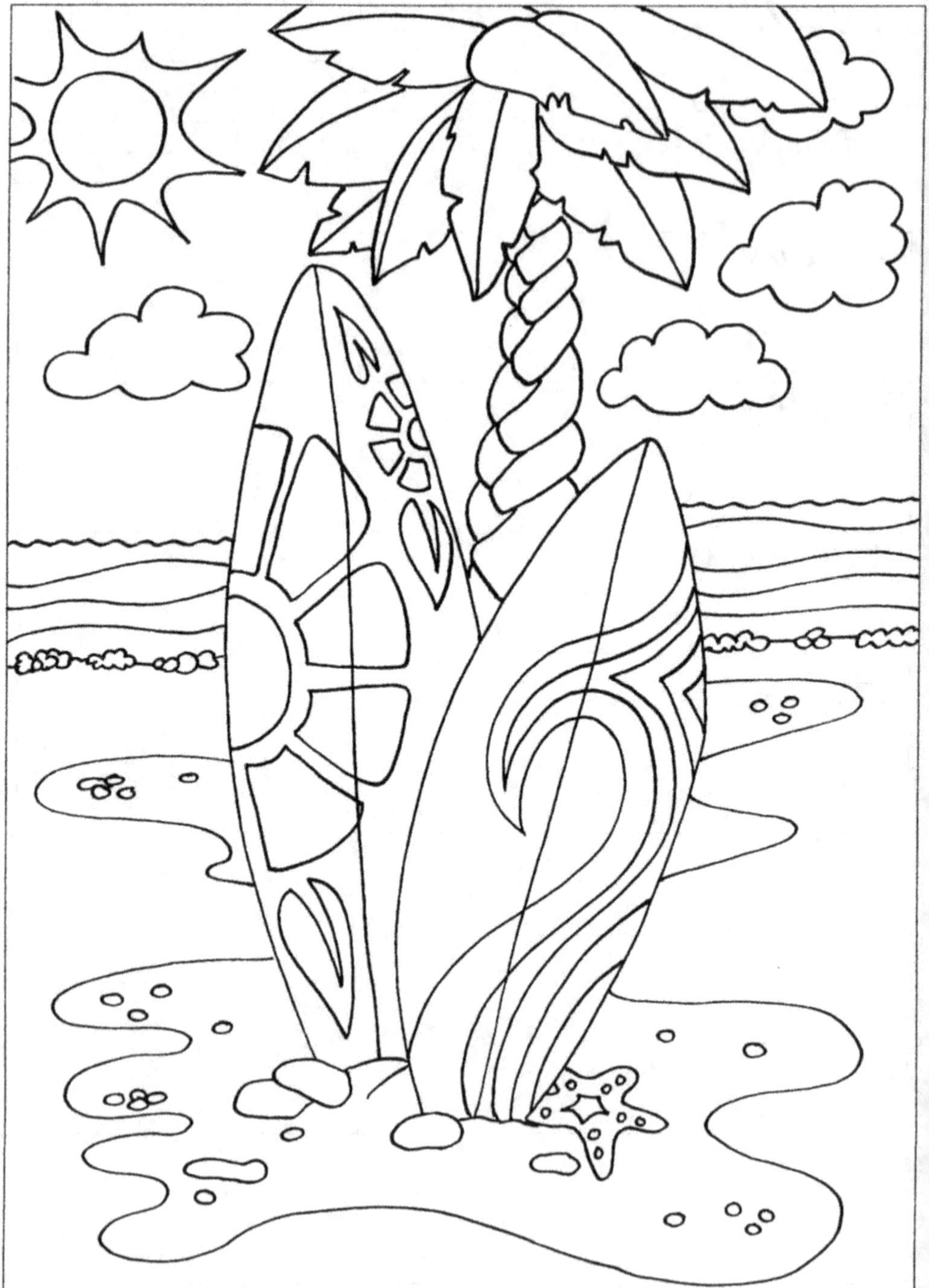

July

WEEK _____

M	T	W	T	F	S	S

Monday

Tuesday

Wednesday

Thursday

Friday

Saturday

Sunday

Notes

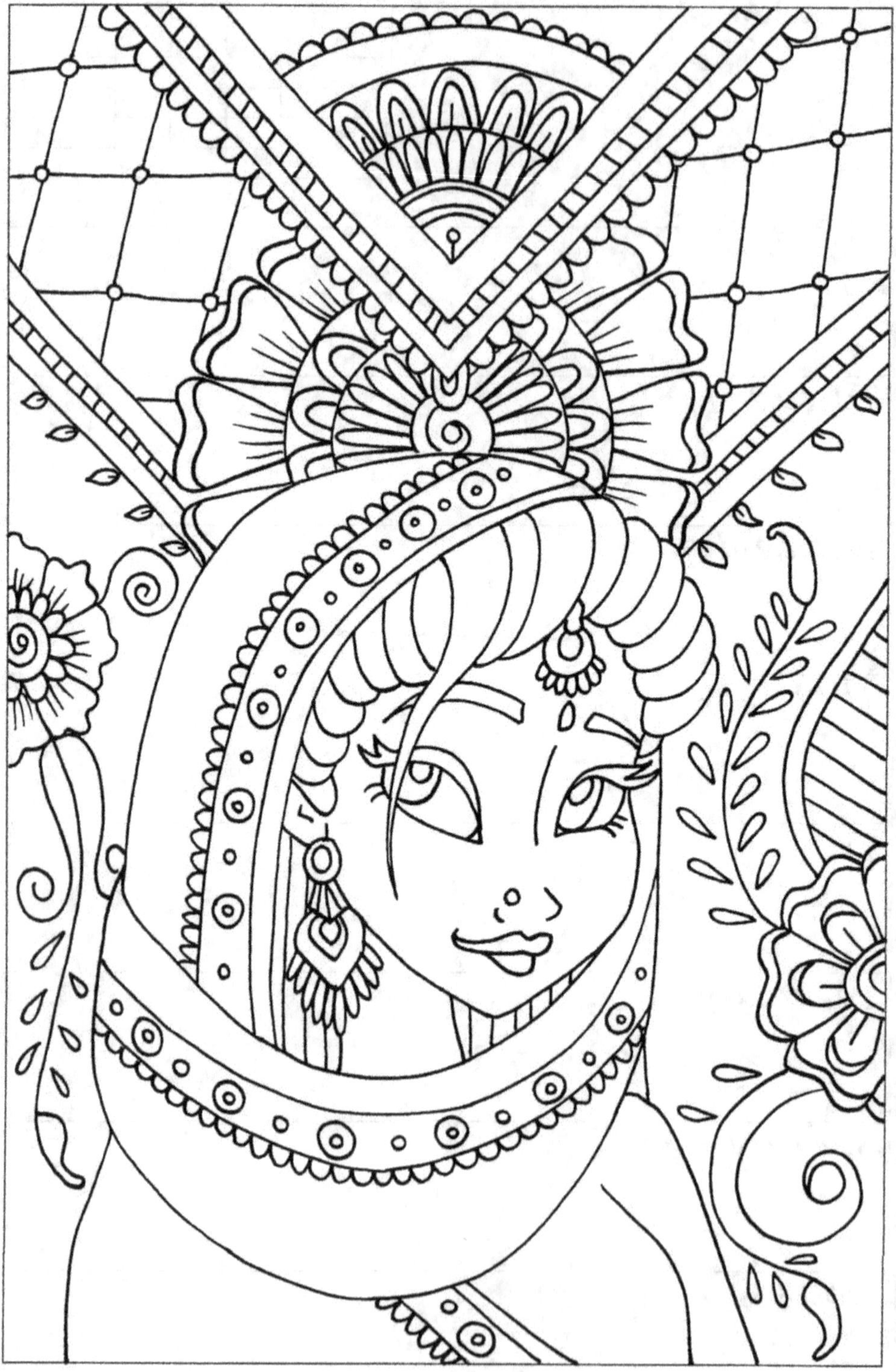

July

WEEK _____

M	T	W	T	F	S	S

Monday

Tuesday

Wednesday

Thursday

Friday

Saturday

Sunday

Notes

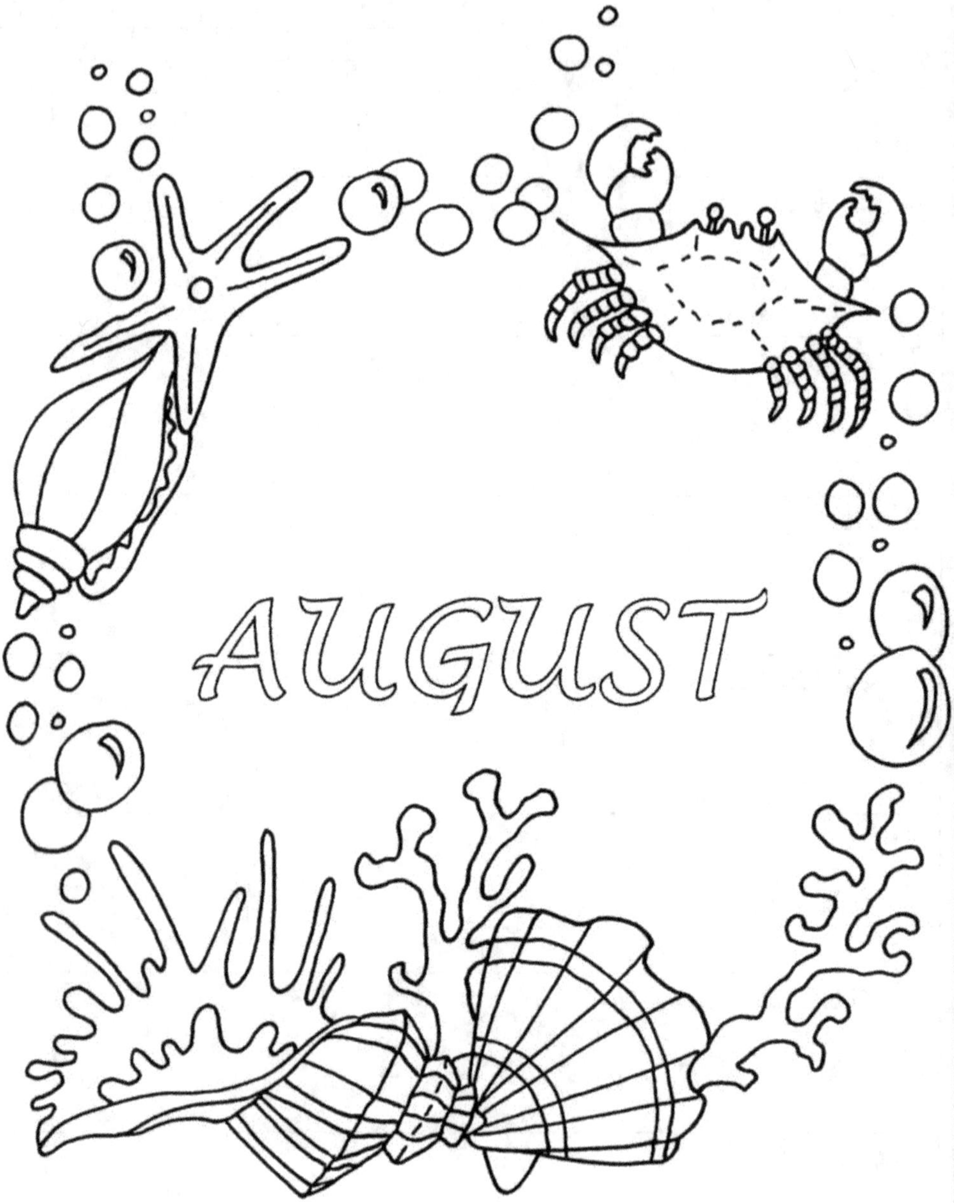
AUGUST

Month at a glance ...

August

M	T	W	T	F	S	S

August To Do:

- ○ ------------------------------------
- ○ ------------------------------------
- ○ ------------------------------------
- ○ ------------------------------------
- ○ ------------------------------------
- ○ ------------------------------------
- ○ ------------------------------------
- ○ ------------------------------------
- ○ ------------------------------------

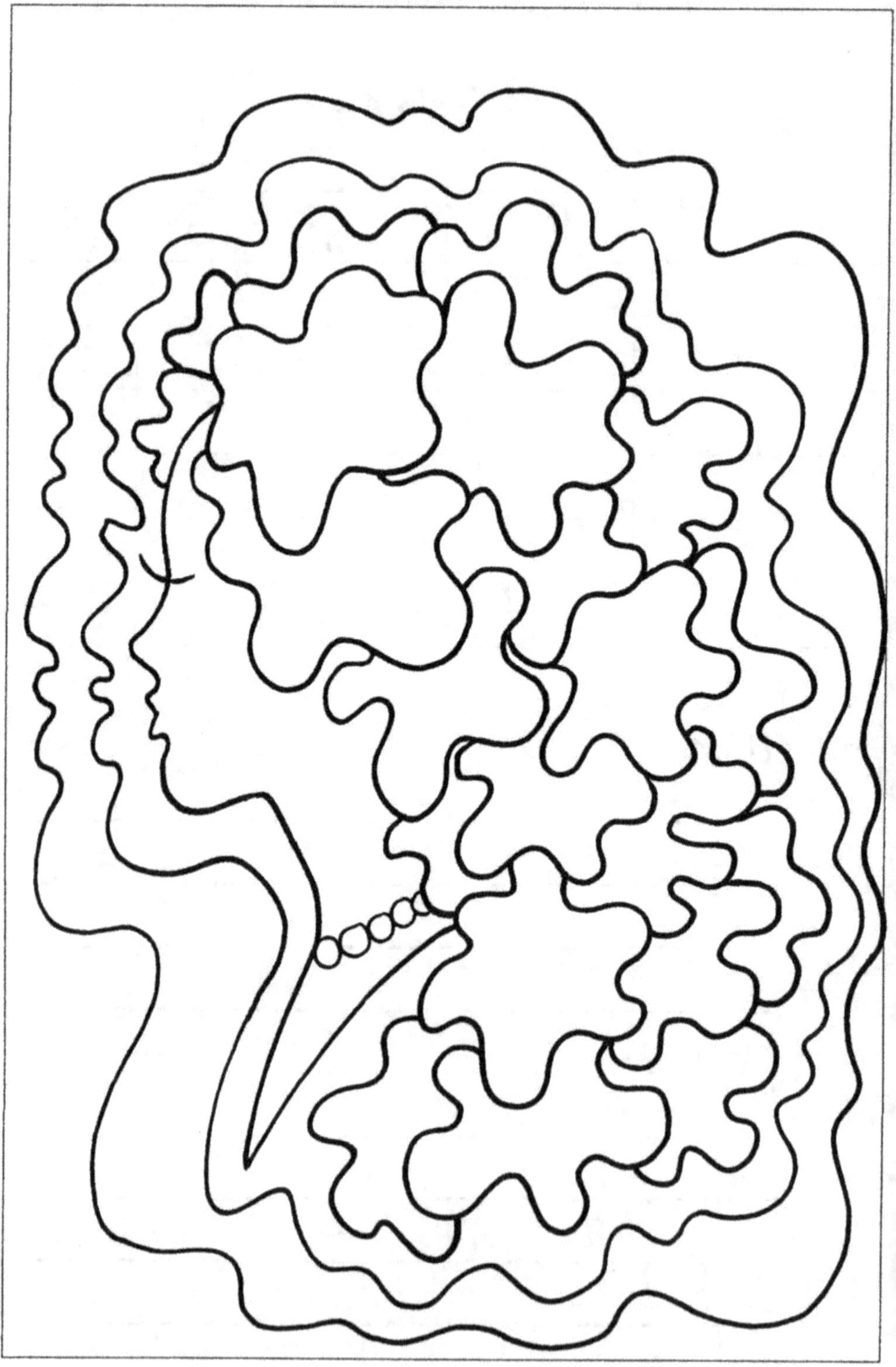

August

WEEK _____

M	T	W	T	F	S	S

Monday

Tuesday

Wednesday

Thursday

Friday

Saturday

Sunday

Notes

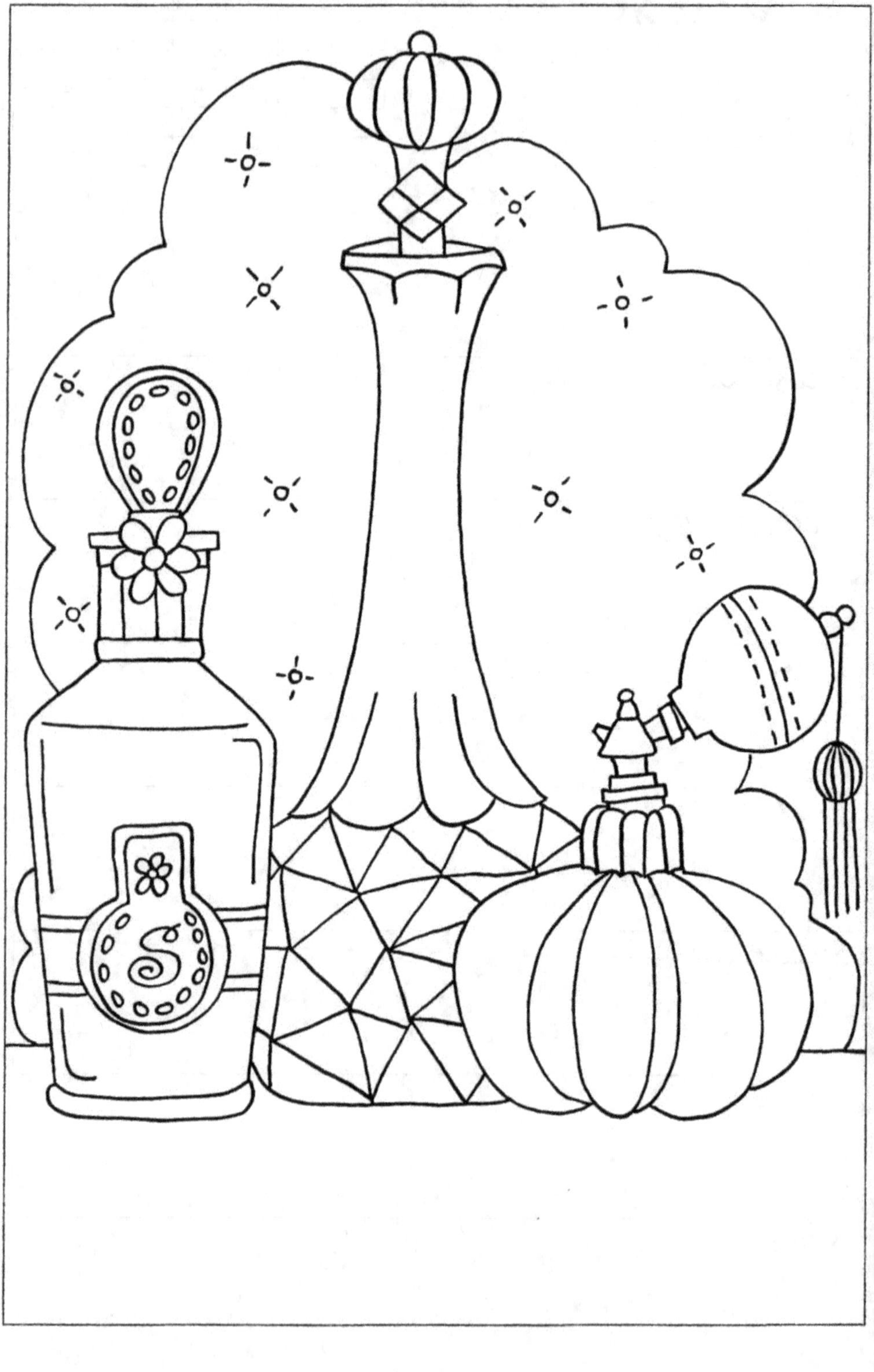

August

WEEK _____

M	T	W	T	F	S	S

Monday
Tuesday
Wednesday
Thursday
Friday
Saturday
Sunday
Notes

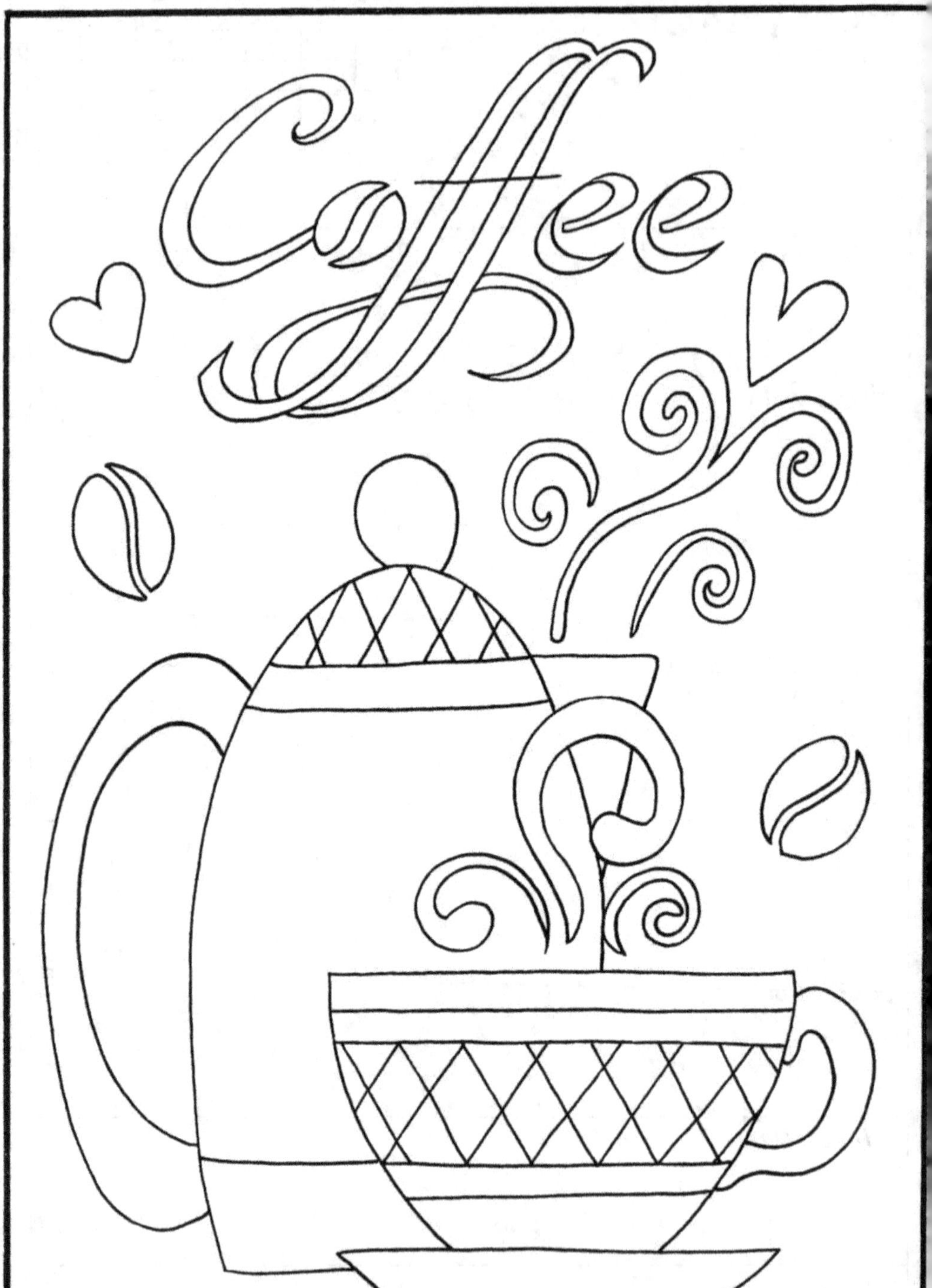
Coffee

August

WEEK _____

M	T	W	T	F	S	S

Monday

Tuesday

Wednesday

Thursday

Friday

Saturday

Sunday

Notes

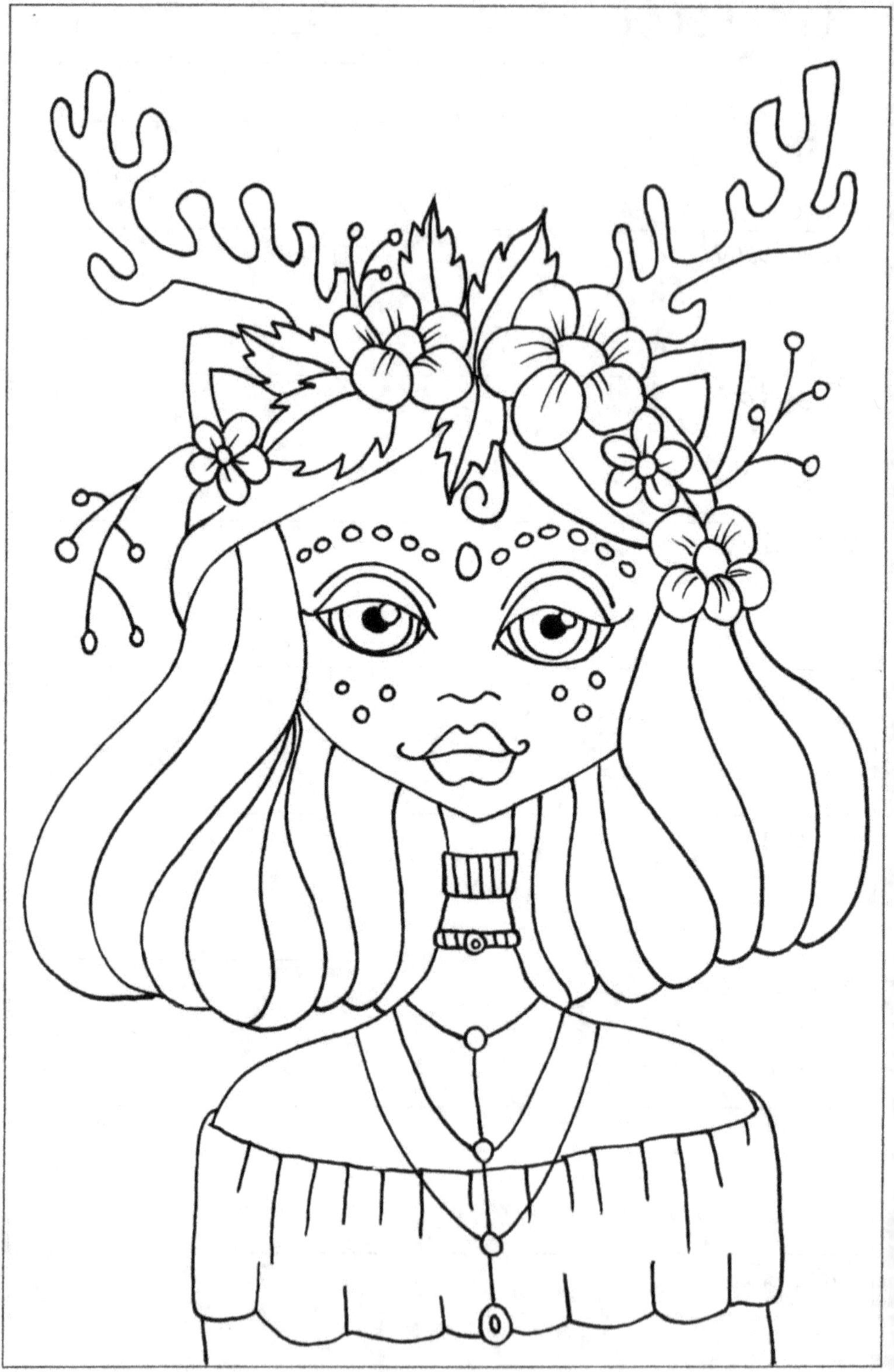

August

WEEK _____

M	T	W	T	F	S	S

Monday

Tuesday

Wednesday

Thursday

Friday

Saturday

Sunday

Notes

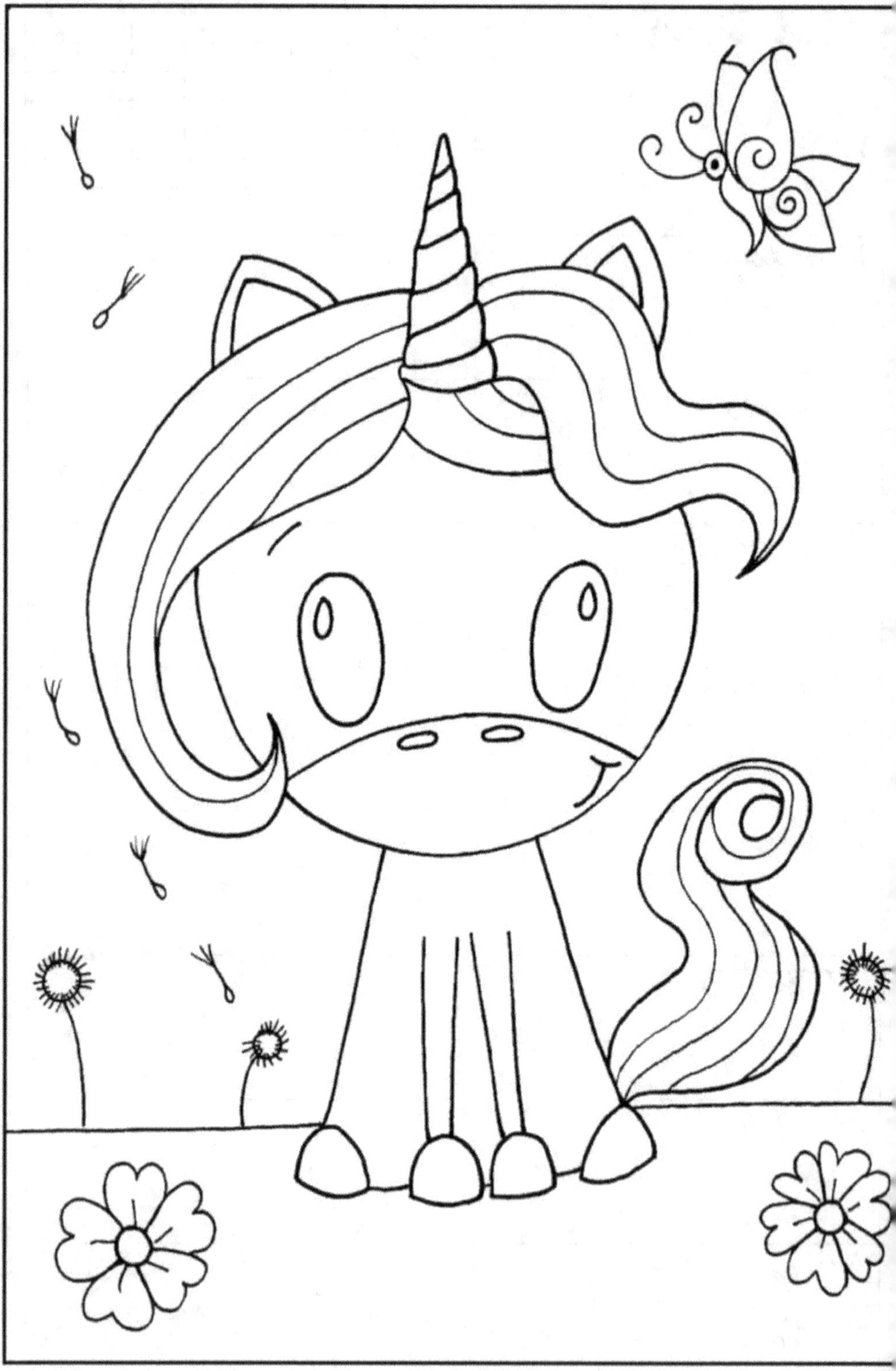

August

WEEK _____

M	T	W	T	F	S	S

Monday
Tuesday
Wednesday
Thursday
Friday
Saturday
Sunday
Notes

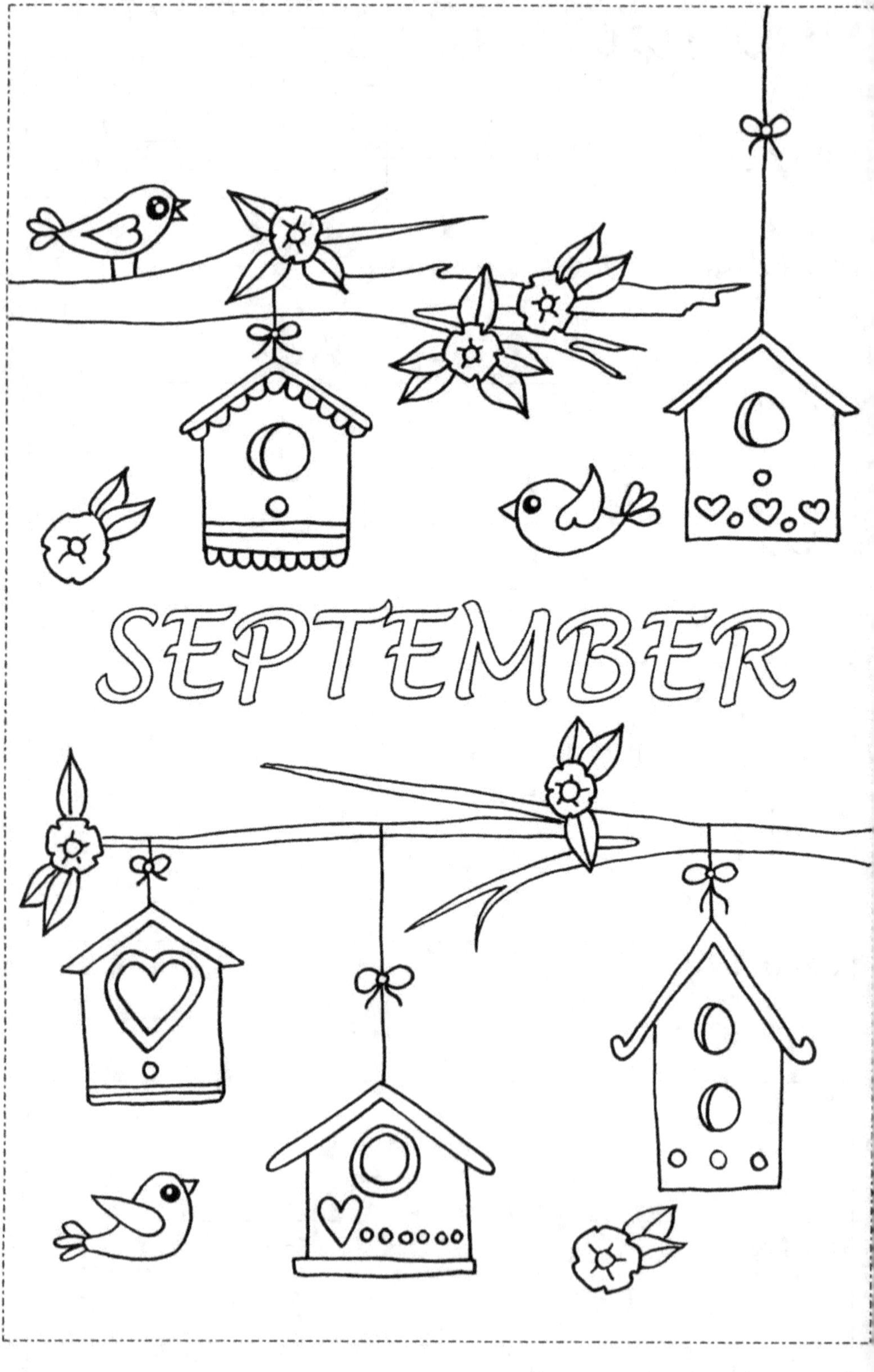
SEPTEMBER

Month at a glance ...

September

M	T	W	T	F	S	S

September To Do:

- ○ ________________________________
- ○ ________________________________
- ○ ________________________________
- ○ ________________________________
- ○ ________________________________
- ○ ________________________________
- ○ ________________________________
- ○ ________________________________
- ○ ________________________________

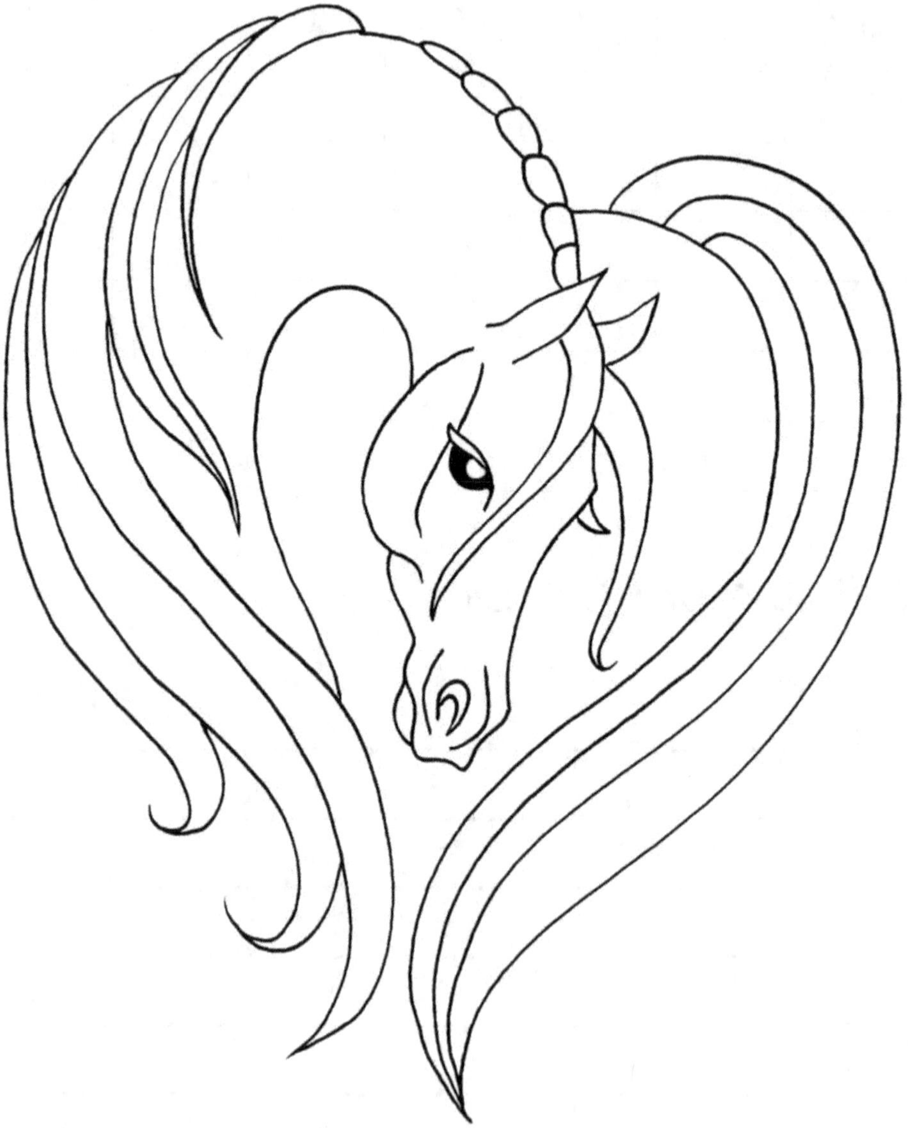

September

WEEK _____

M	T	W	T	F	S	S

Monday

Tuesday

Wednesday

Thursday

Friday

Saturday

Sunday

Notes

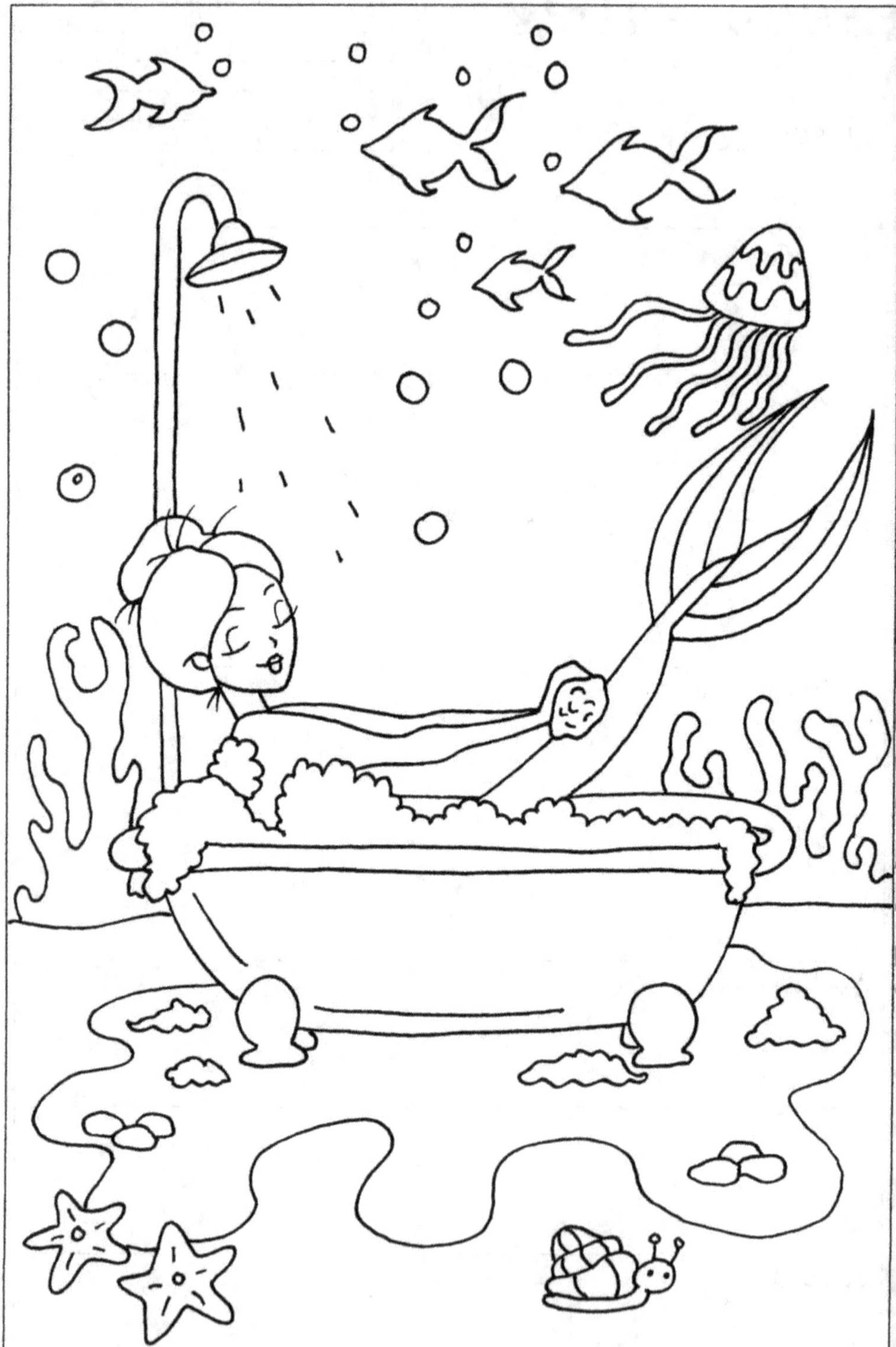

September

WEEK _____

M	T	W	T	F	S	S

Monday

Tuesday

Wednesday

Thursday

Friday

Saturday

Sunday

Notes

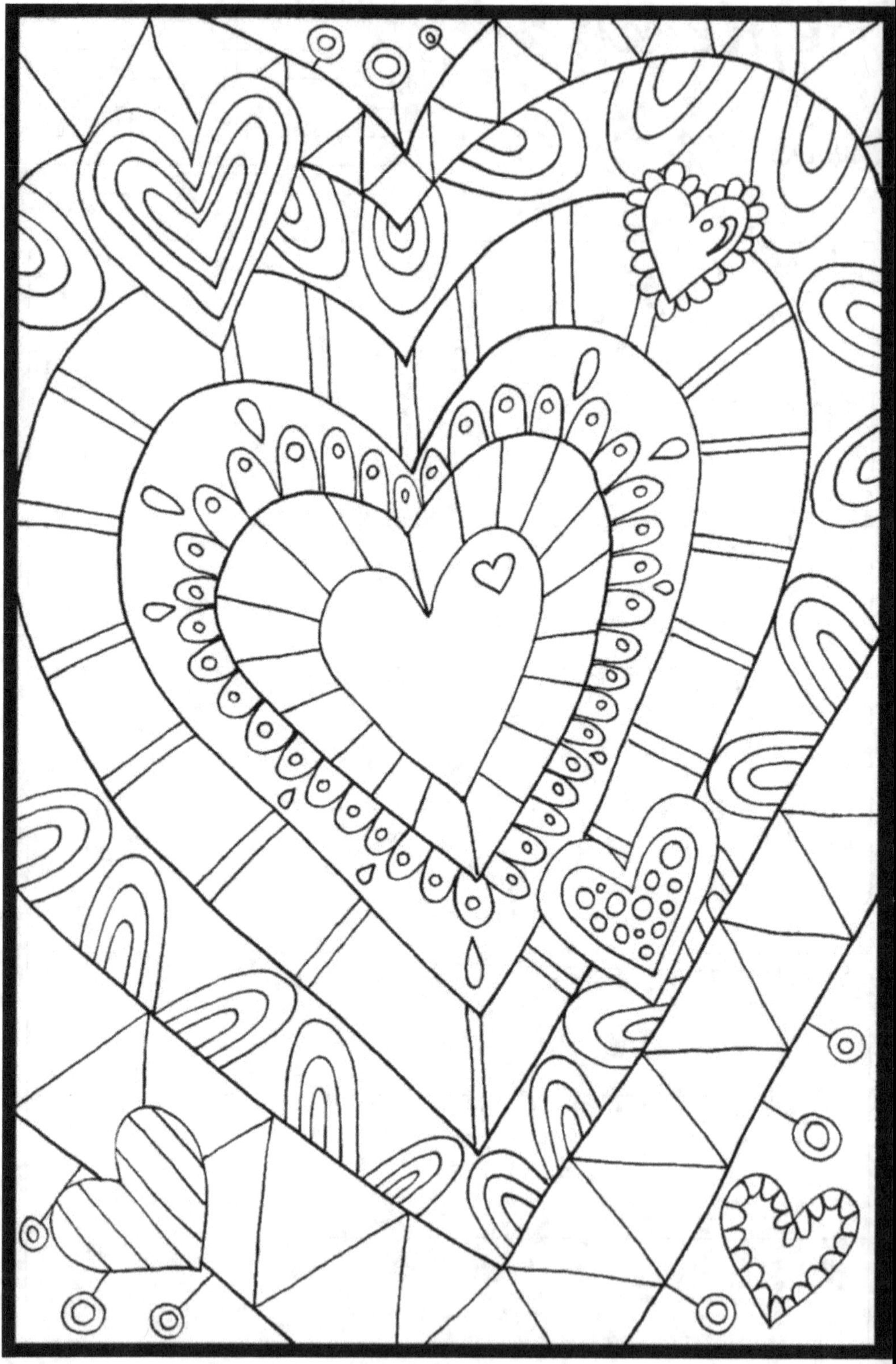

September

WEEK _____

M	T	W	T	F	S	S

Monday

Tuesday

Wednesday

Thursday

Friday

Saturday

Sunday

Notes

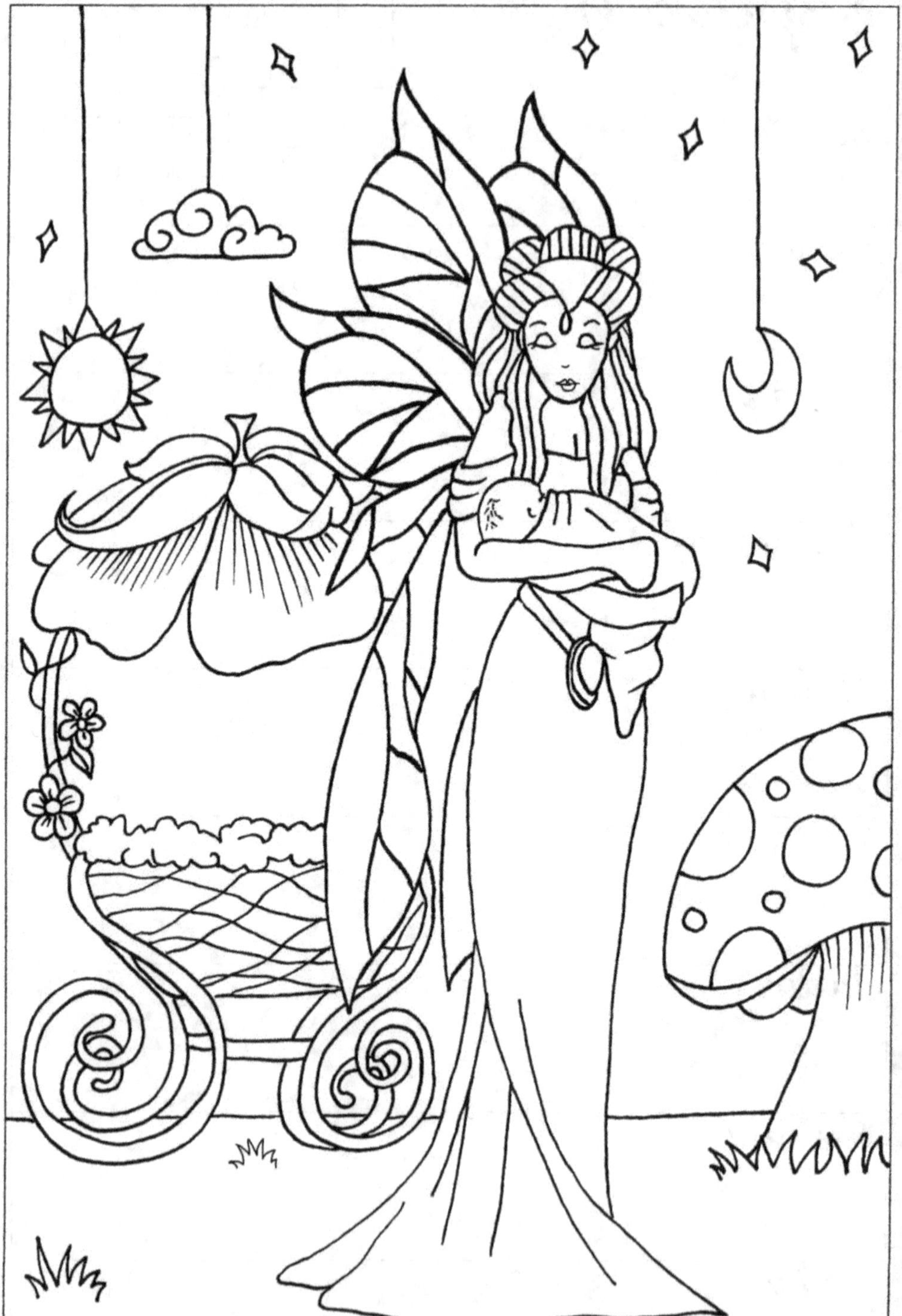

September

WEEK _____

M	T	W	T	F	S	S

Monday
Tuesday
Wednesday
Thursday
Friday
Saturday
Sunday
Notes

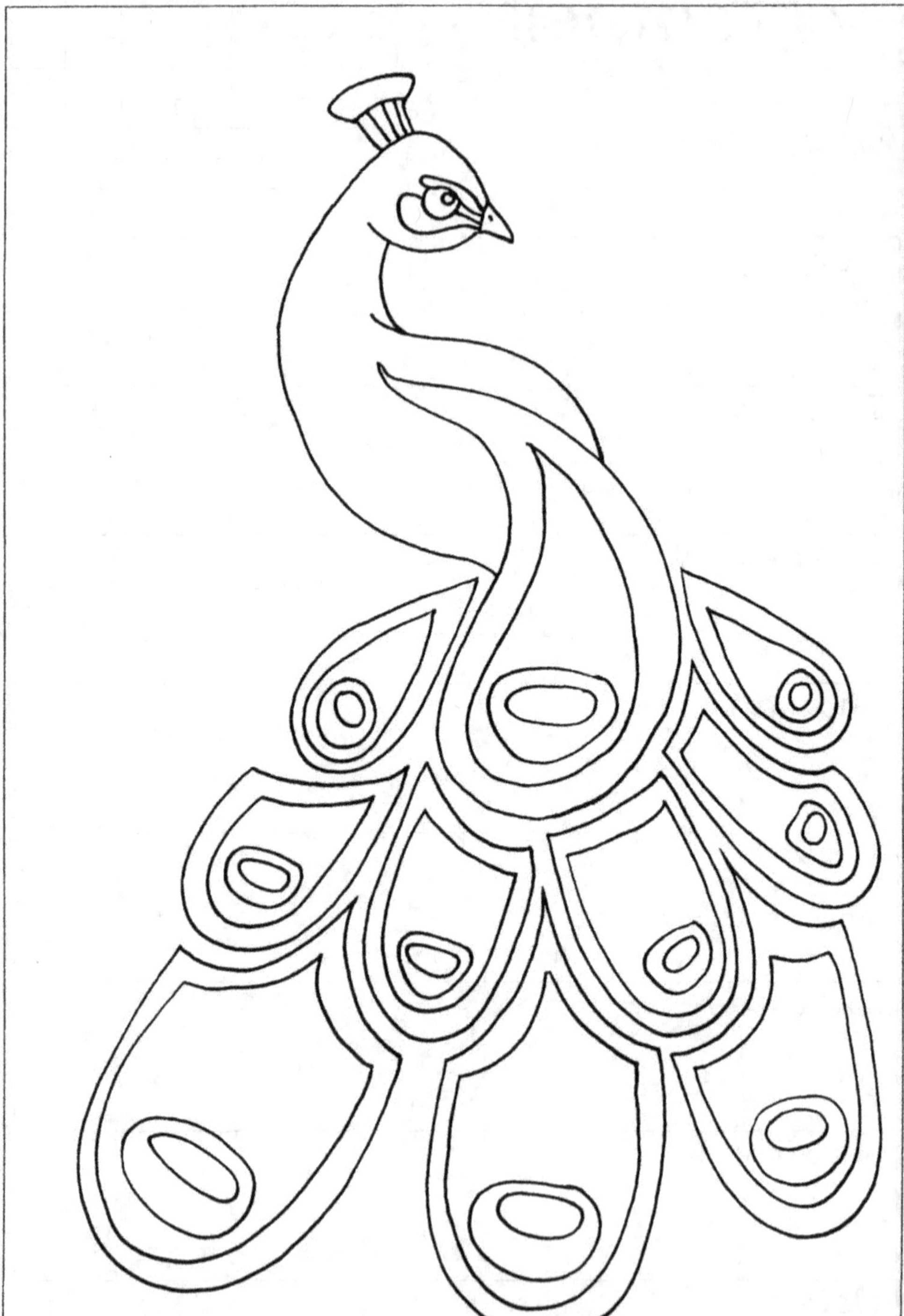

September

WEEK _____

M	T	W	T	F	S	S

Monday

Tuesday

Wednesday

Thursday

Friday

Saturday

Sunday

Notes

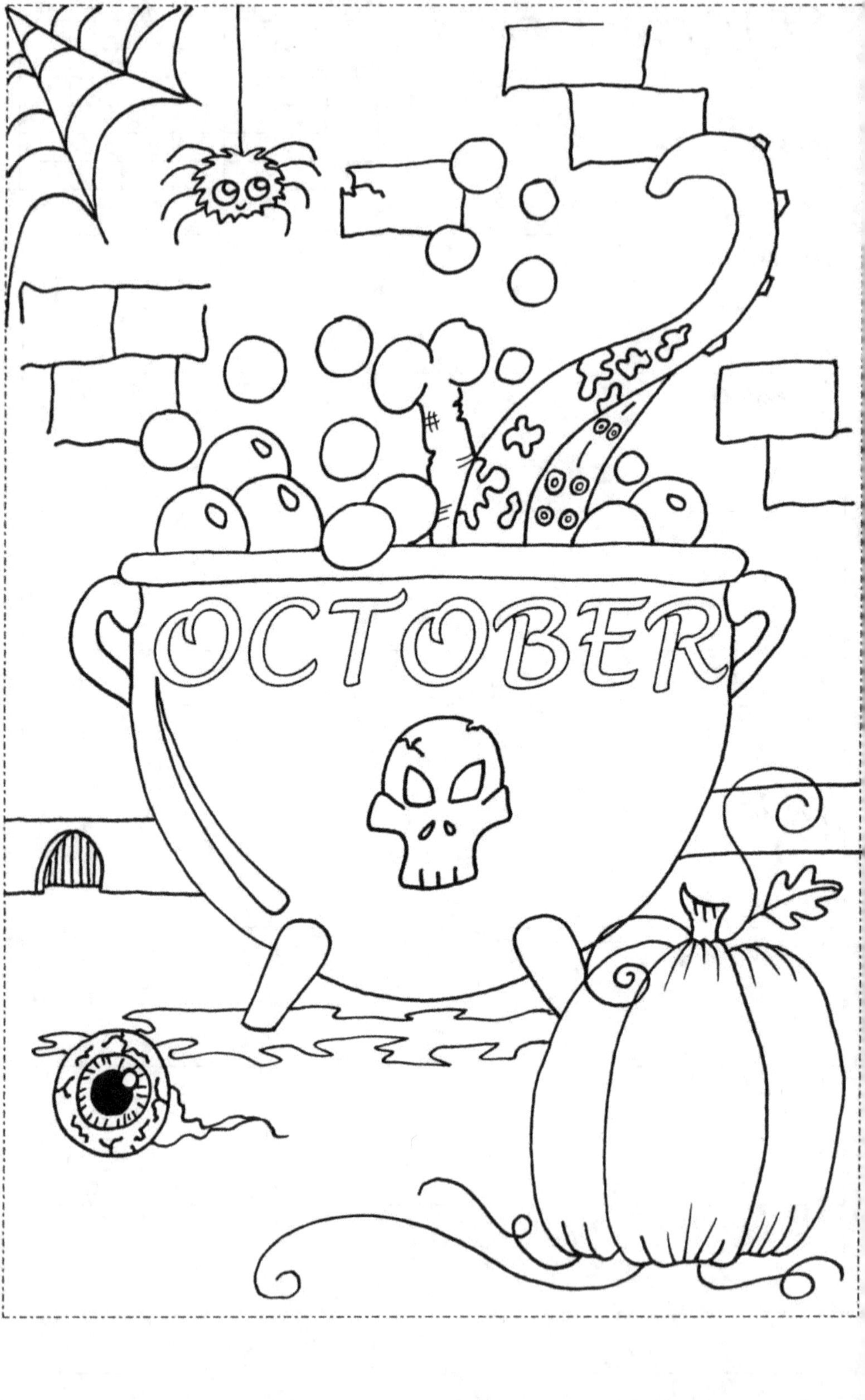
OCTOBER

Month at a glance …

October

M	T	W	T	F	S	S

October To Do:

- ○ ______________________________
- ○ ______________________________
- ○ ______________________________
- ○ ______________________________
- ○ ______________________________
- ○ ______________________________
- ○ ______________________________
- ○ ______________________________
- ○ ______________________________

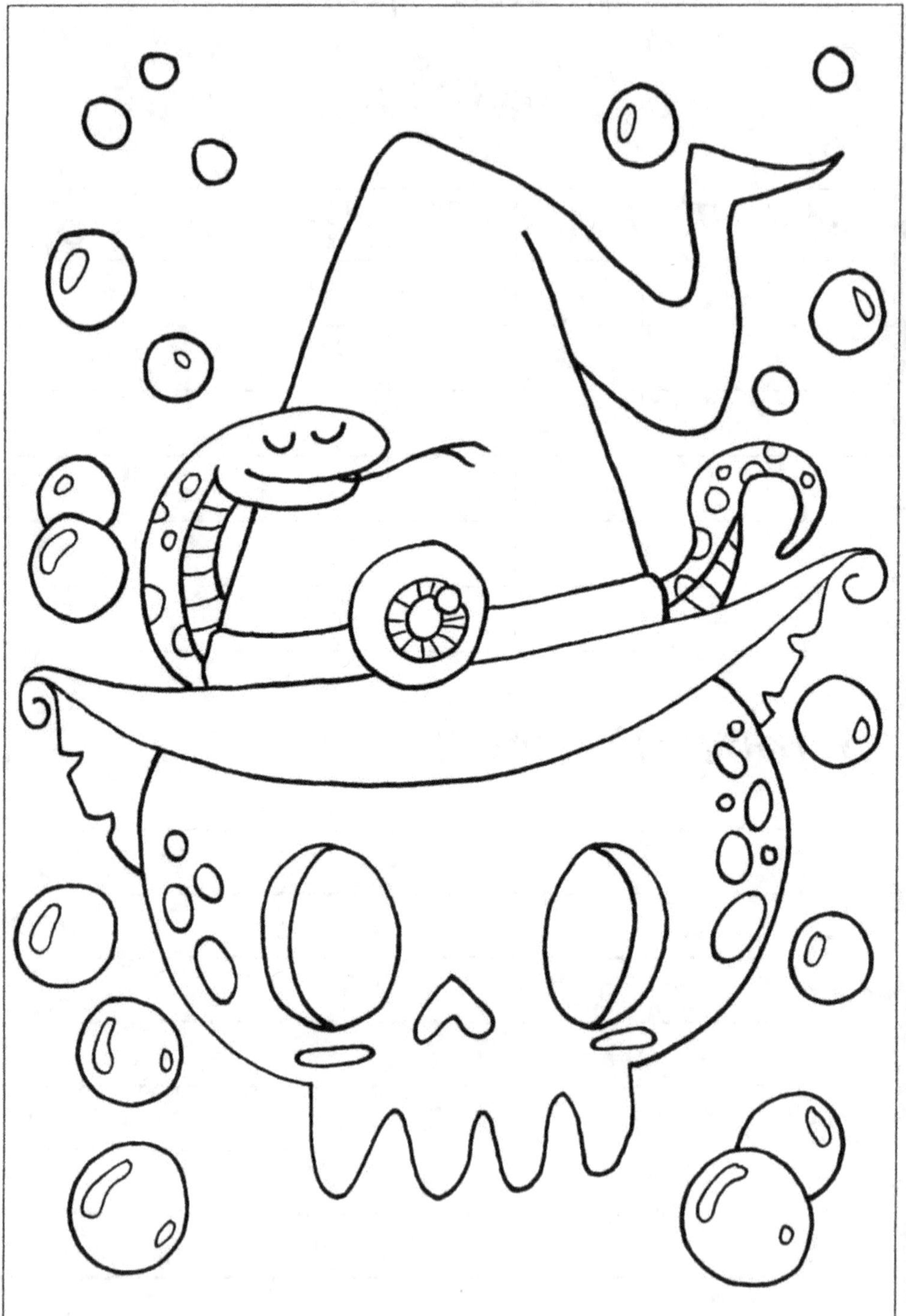

October

WEEK _____

M	T	W	T	F	S	S

Monday

Tuesday

Wednesday

Thursday

Friday

Saturday

Sunday

Notes

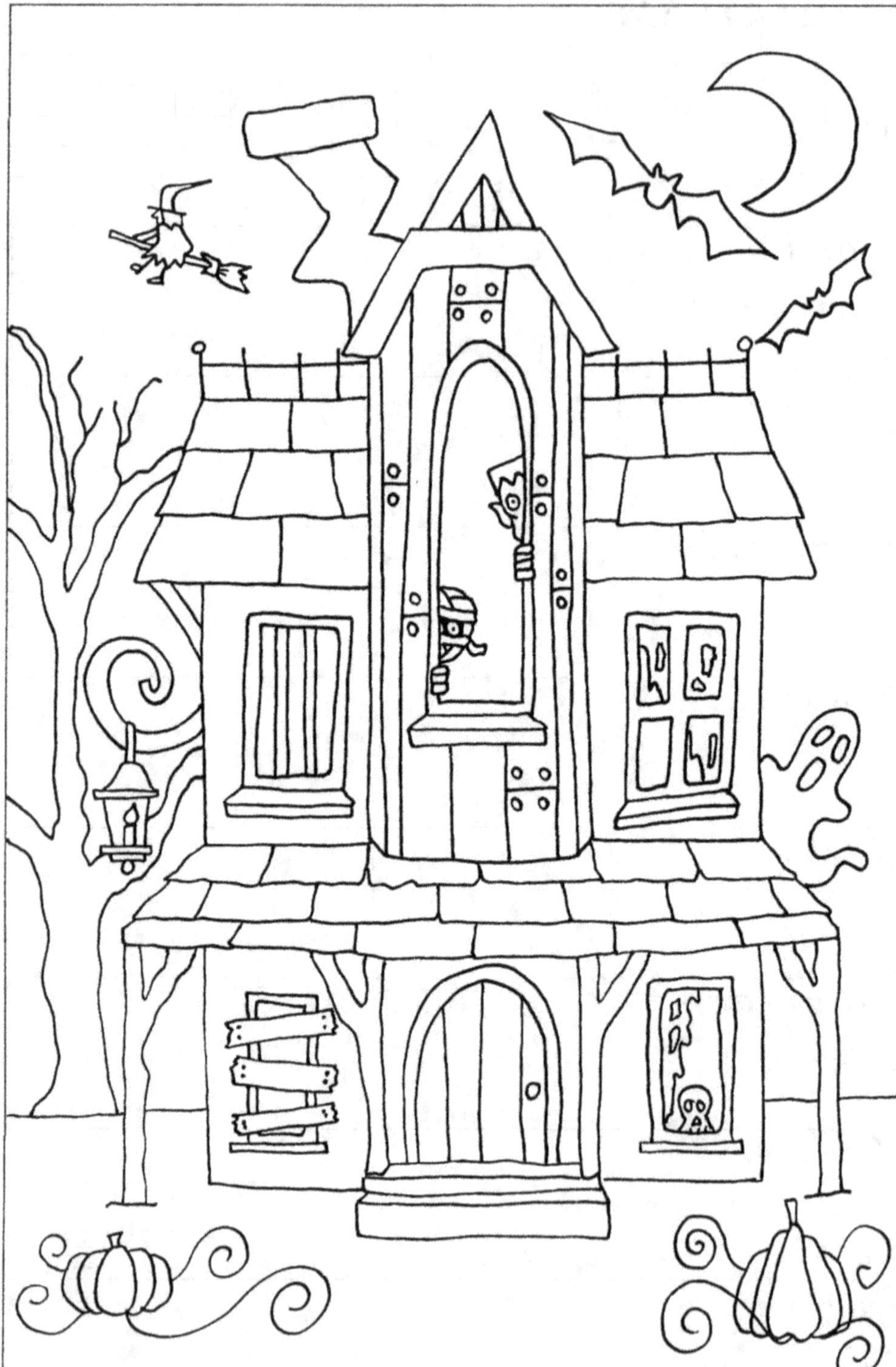

October

WEEK _____

M	T	W	T	F	S	S

Monday

Tuesday

Wednesday

Thursday

Friday

Saturday

Sunday

Notes

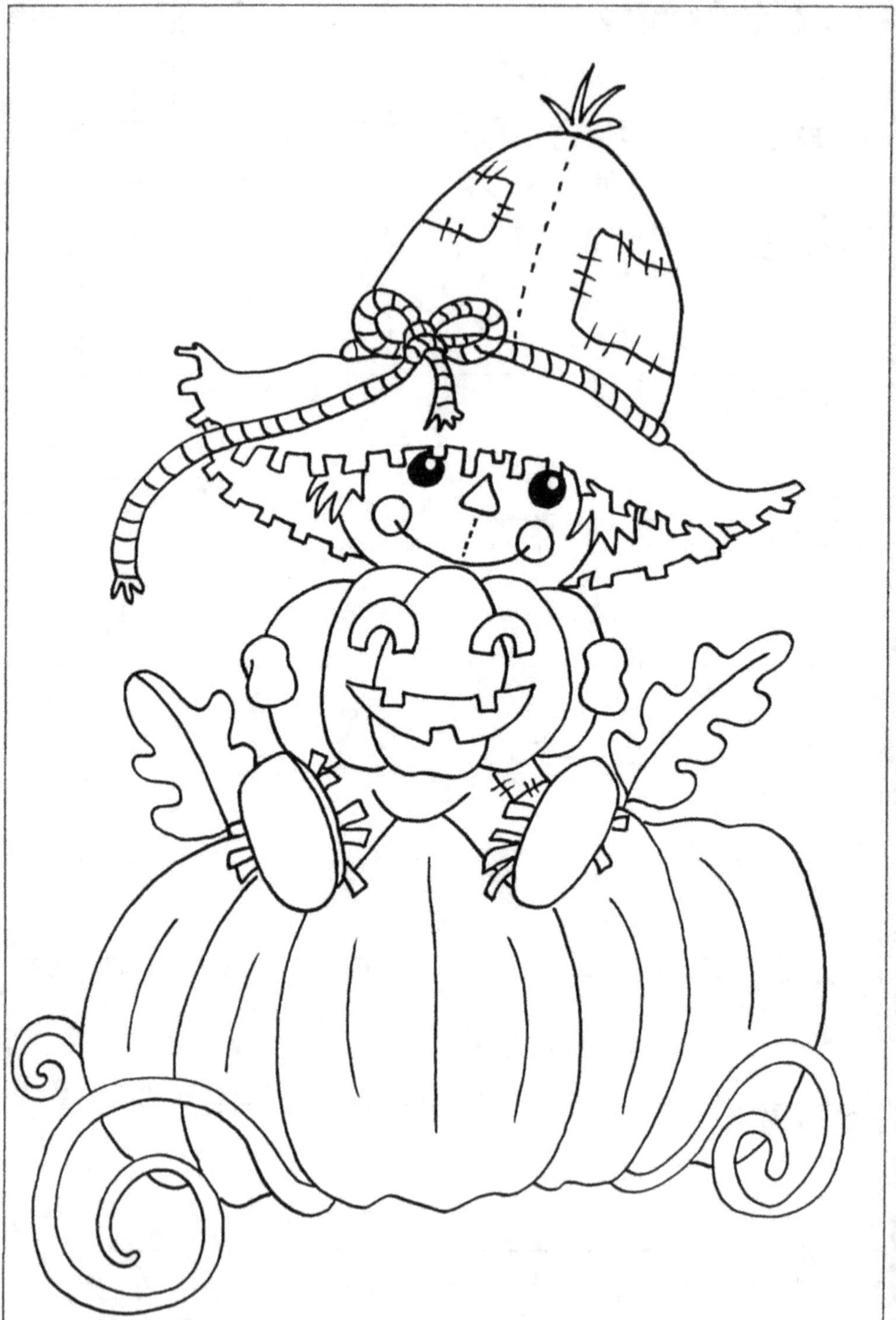

October

WEEK _____

M	T	W	T	F	S	S

Monday

Tuesday

Wednesday

Thursday

Friday

Saturday

Sunday

Notes

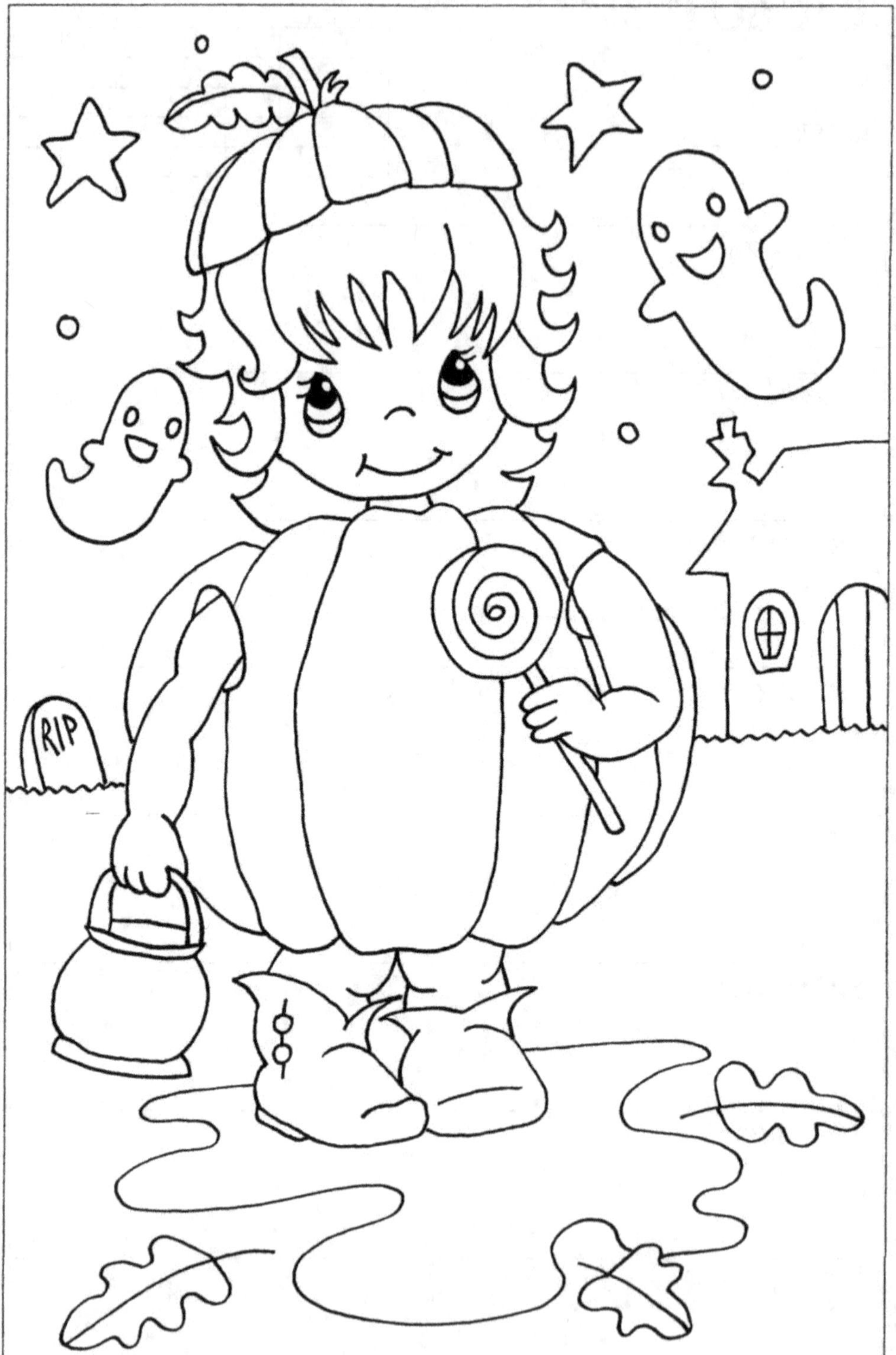
RIP

October

WEEK _____

M	T	W	T	F	S	S

Monday

Tuesday

Wednesday

Thursday

Friday

Saturday

Sunday

Notes

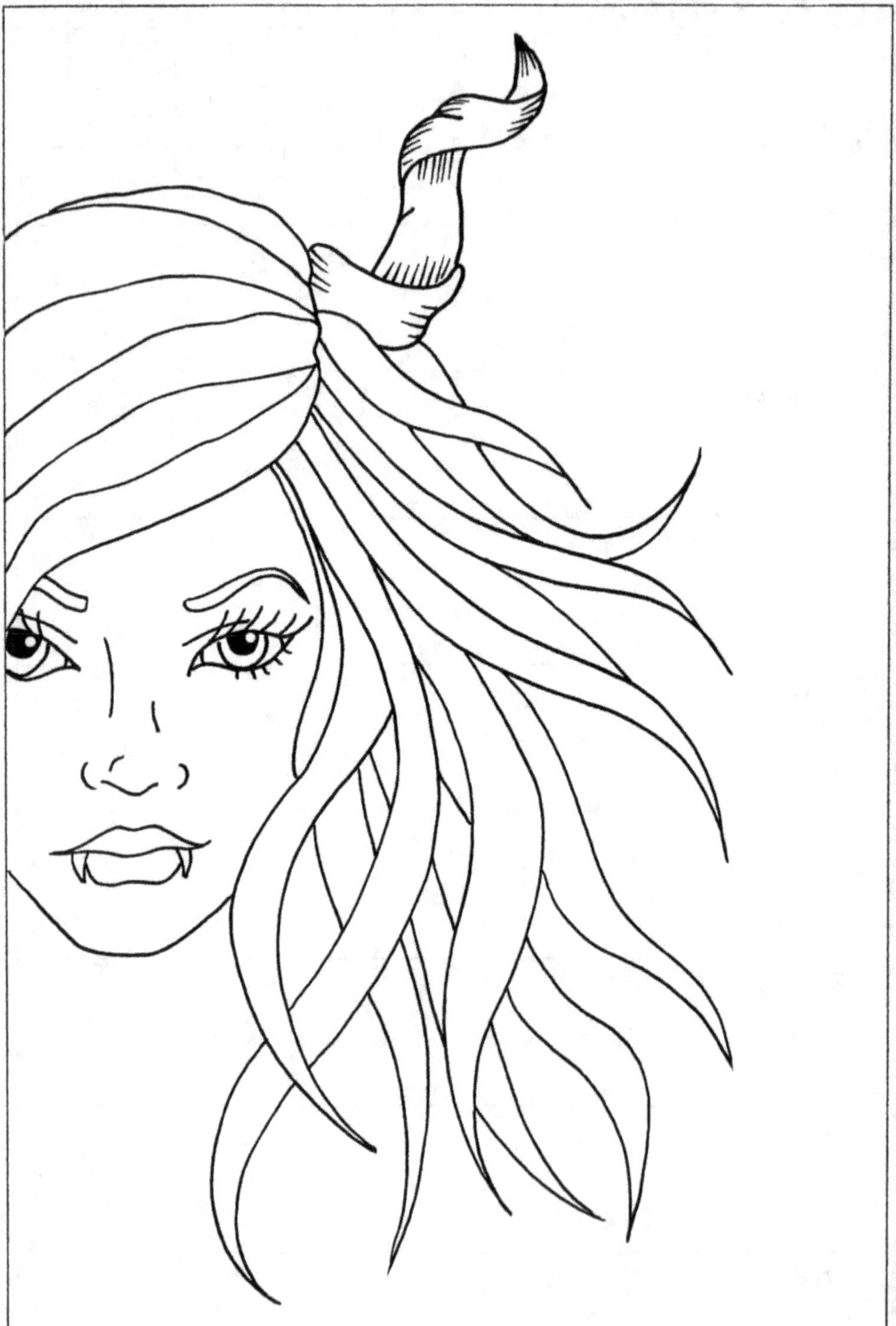

October

WEEK _____

M	T	W	T	F	S	S

Monday

Tuesday

Wednesday

Thursday

Friday

Saturday

Sunday

Notes

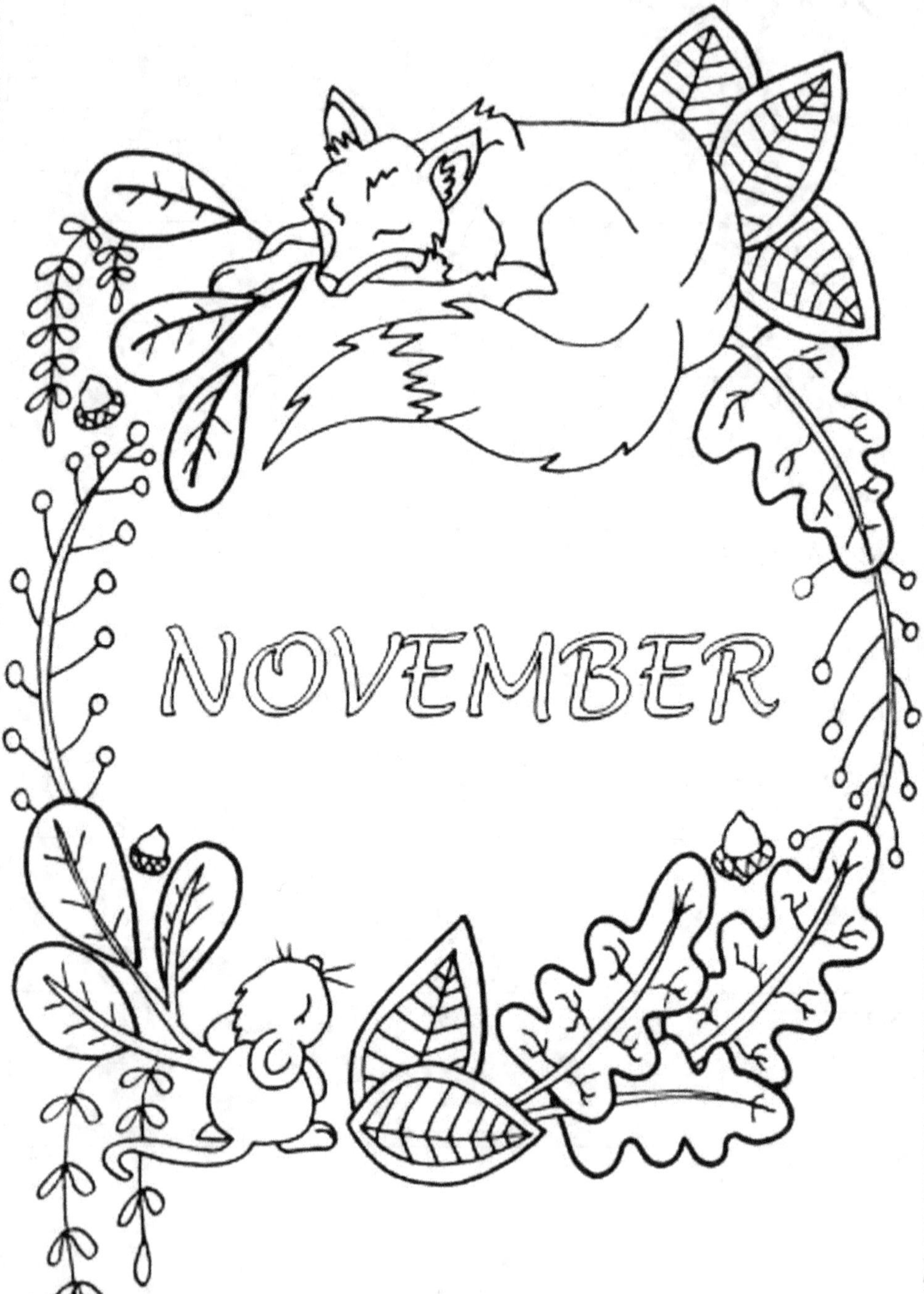
NOVEMBER

Month at a glance ...

November

M	T	W	T	F	S	S

November To Do:

- ○ ___________________________________
- ○ ___________________________________
- ○ ___________________________________
- ○ ___________________________________
- ○ ___________________________________
- ○ ___________________________________
- ○ ___________________________________
- ○ ___________________________________
- ○ ___________________________________

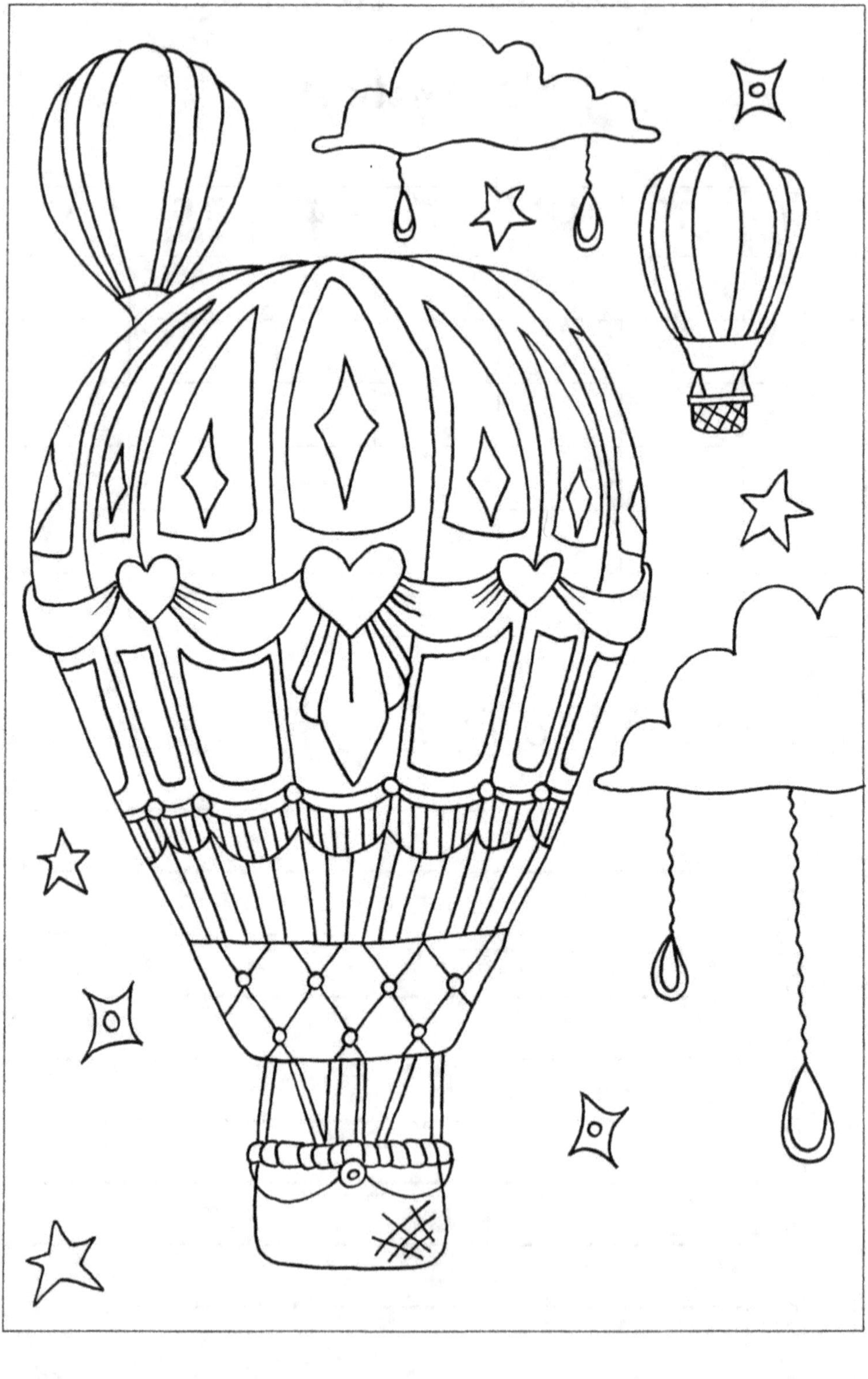

November

WEEK _____

M	T	W	T	F	S	S

Monday
Tuesday
Wednesday
Thursday
Friday
Saturday
Sunday
Notes

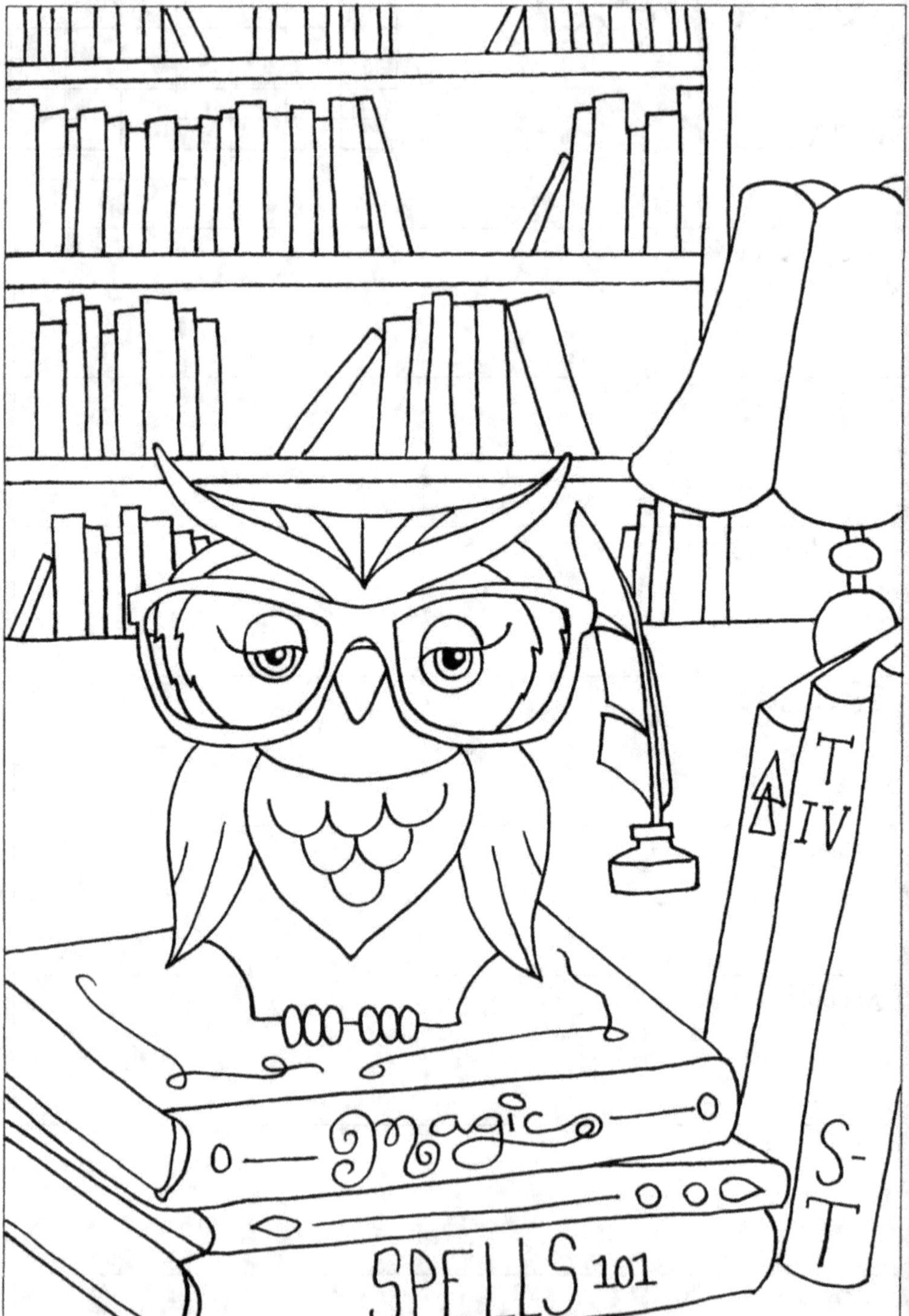
T
IV
S-
T
Magic
SPELLS 101

November

WEEK _____

M	T	W	T	F	S	S

Monday
Tuesday
Wednesday
Thursday
Friday
Saturday
Sunday
Notes

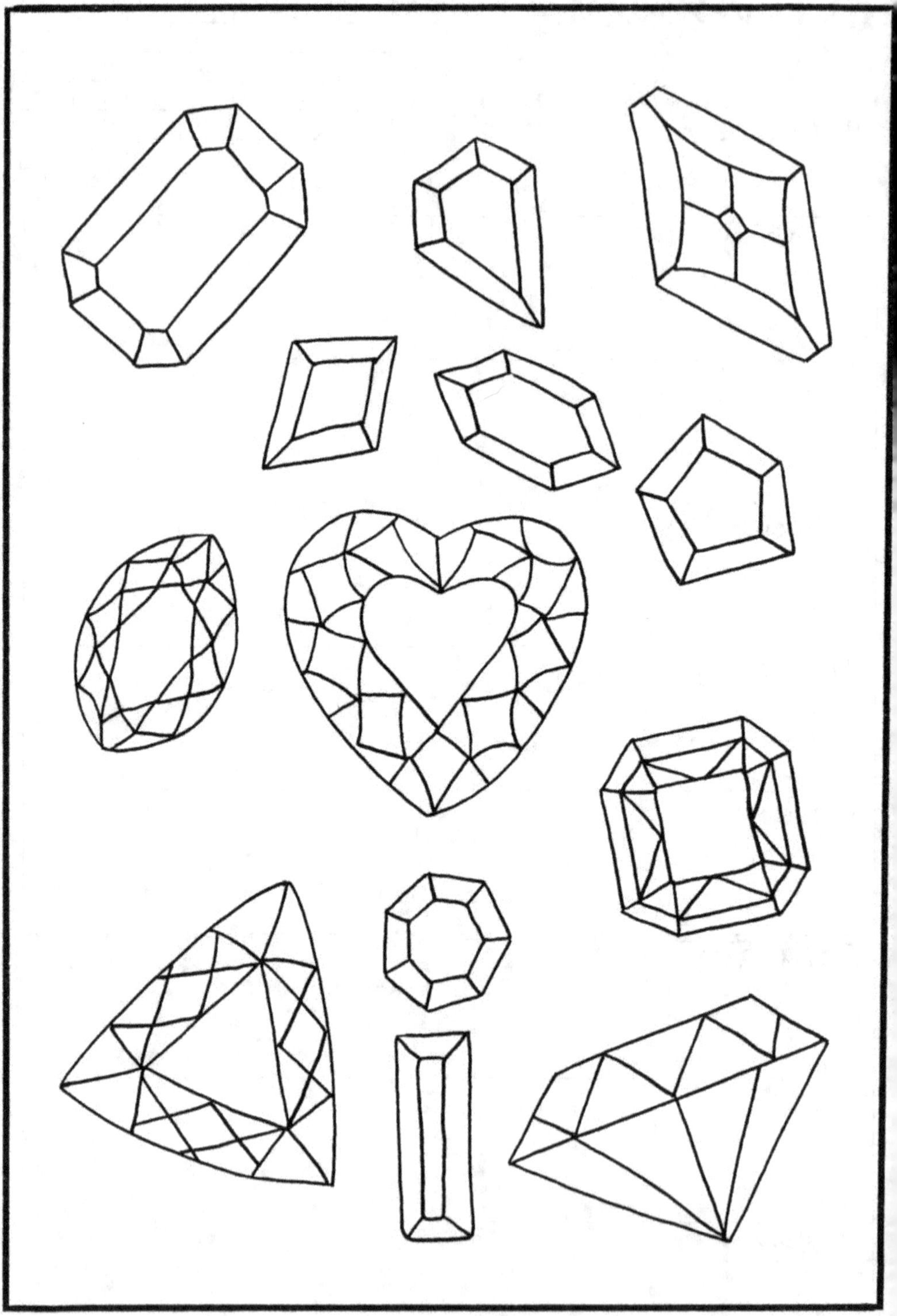

November

WEEK _____

M	T	W	T	F	S	S

Monday

Tuesday

Wednesday

Thursday

Friday

Saturday

Sunday

Notes

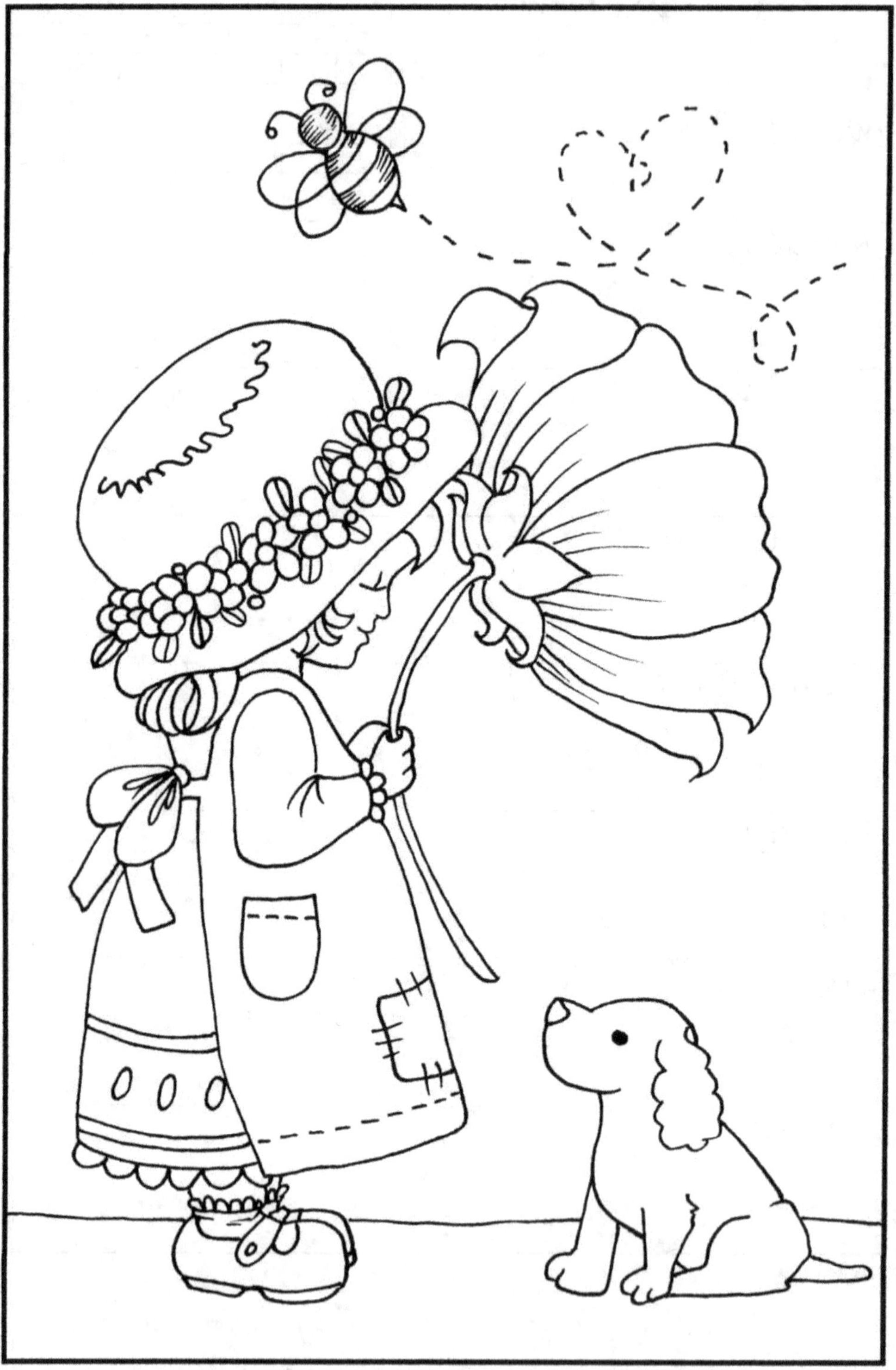

November

WEEK _____

M	T	W	T	F	S	S

Monday

Tuesday

Wednesday

Thursday

Friday

Saturday

Sunday

Notes

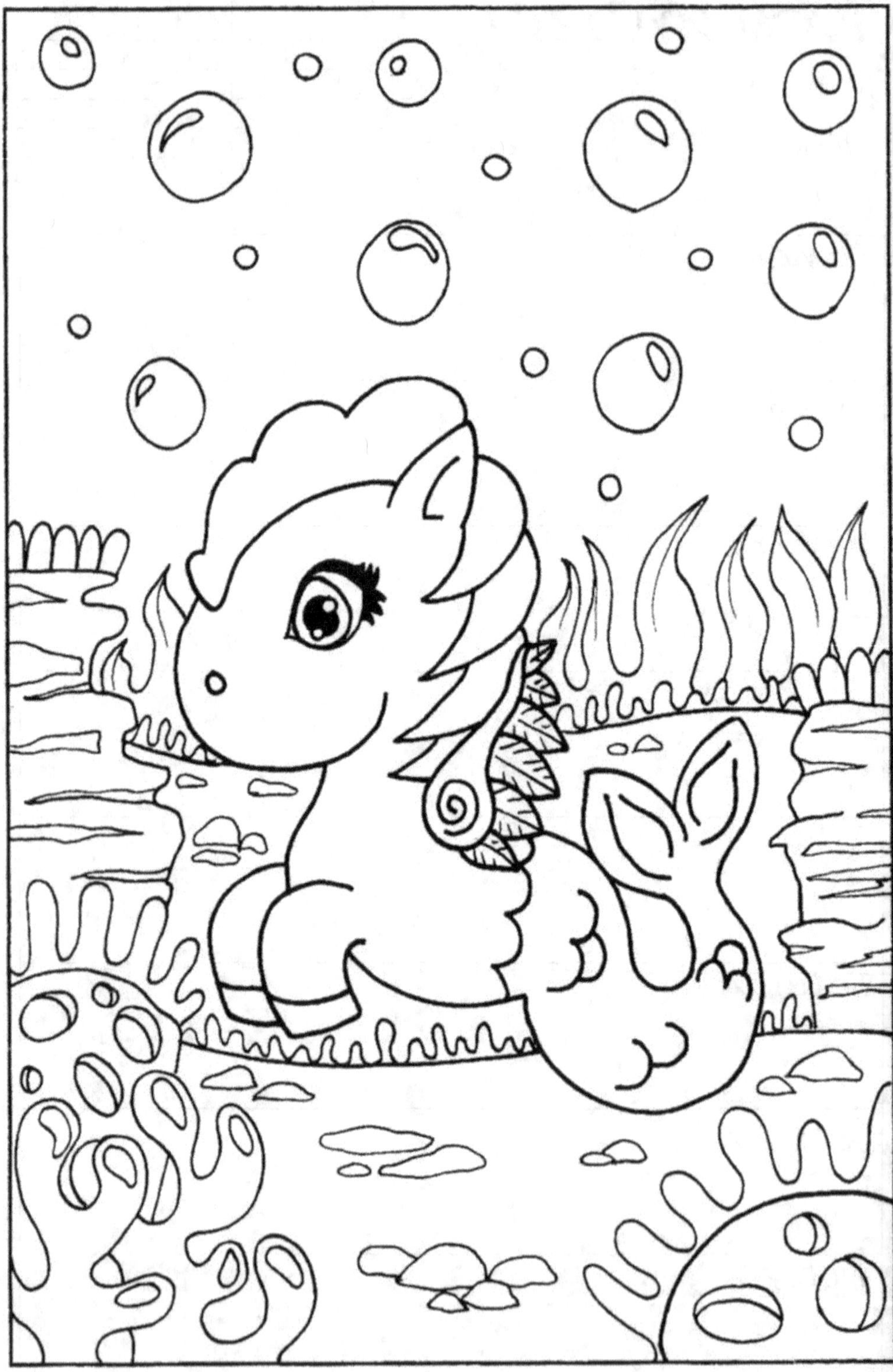

November

WEEK _____

M	T	W	T	F	S	S

Monday

Tuesday

Wednesday

Thursday

Friday

Saturday

Sunday

Notes

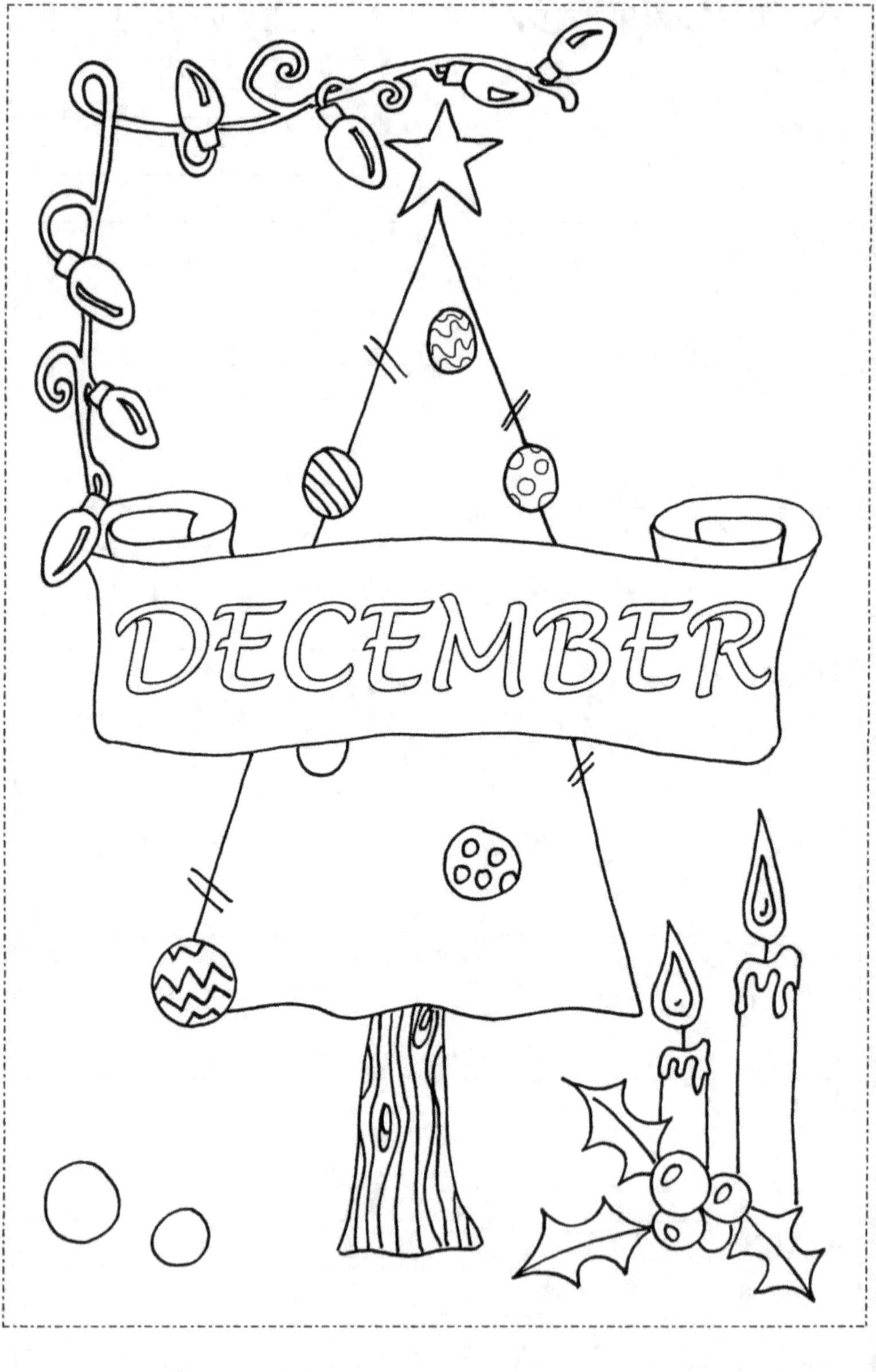
DECEMBER

Month at a glance ...

December

M	T	W	T	F	S	S

December To Do:

- ○ ________________________________
- ○ ________________________________
- ○ ________________________________
- ○ ________________________________
- ○ ________________________________
- ○ ________________________________
- ○ ________________________________
- ○ ________________________________
- ○ ________________________________

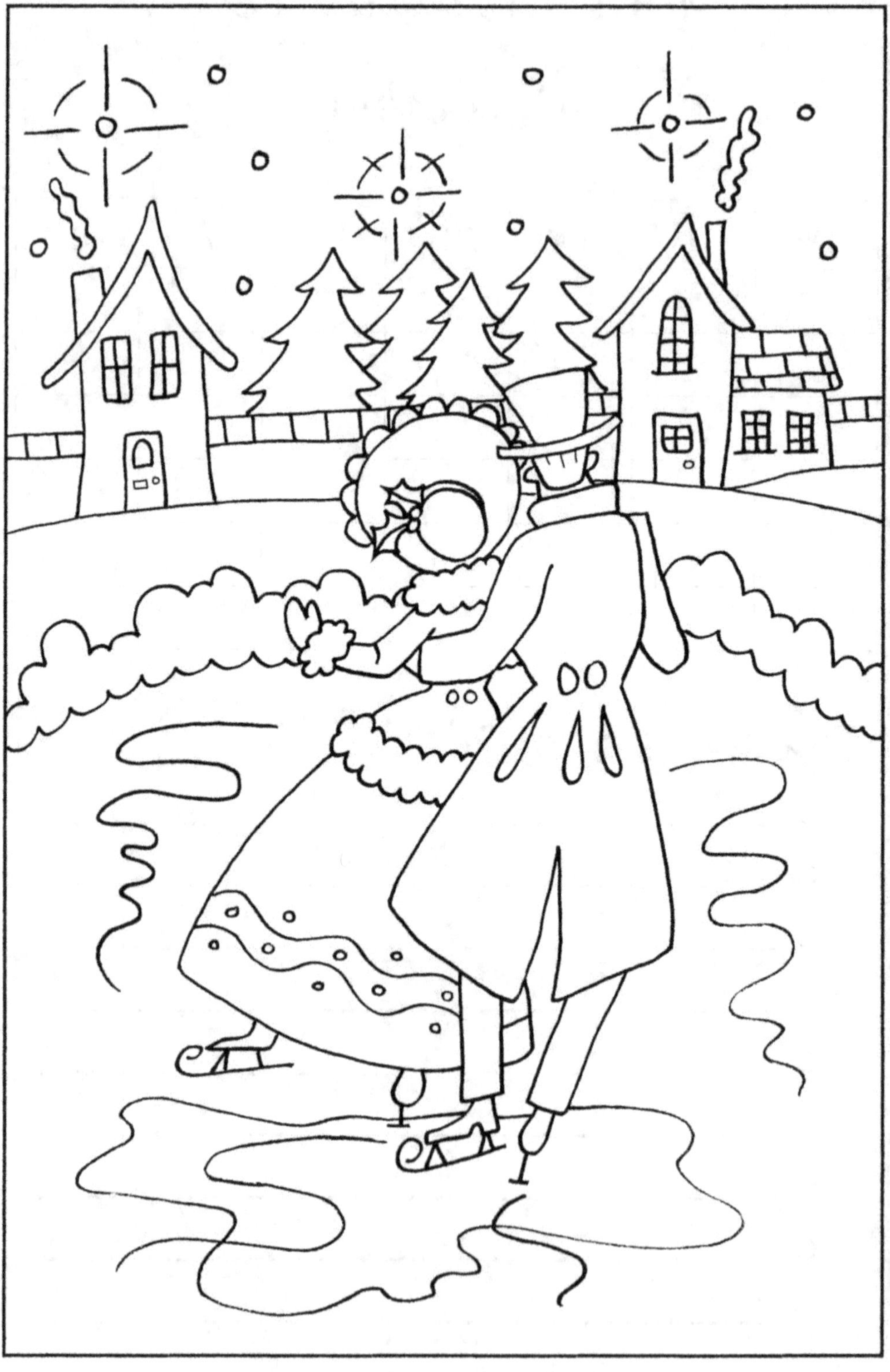

December

WEEK _____

M	T	W	T	F	S	S

Monday

Tuesday

Wednesday

Thursday

Friday

Saturday

Sunday

Notes

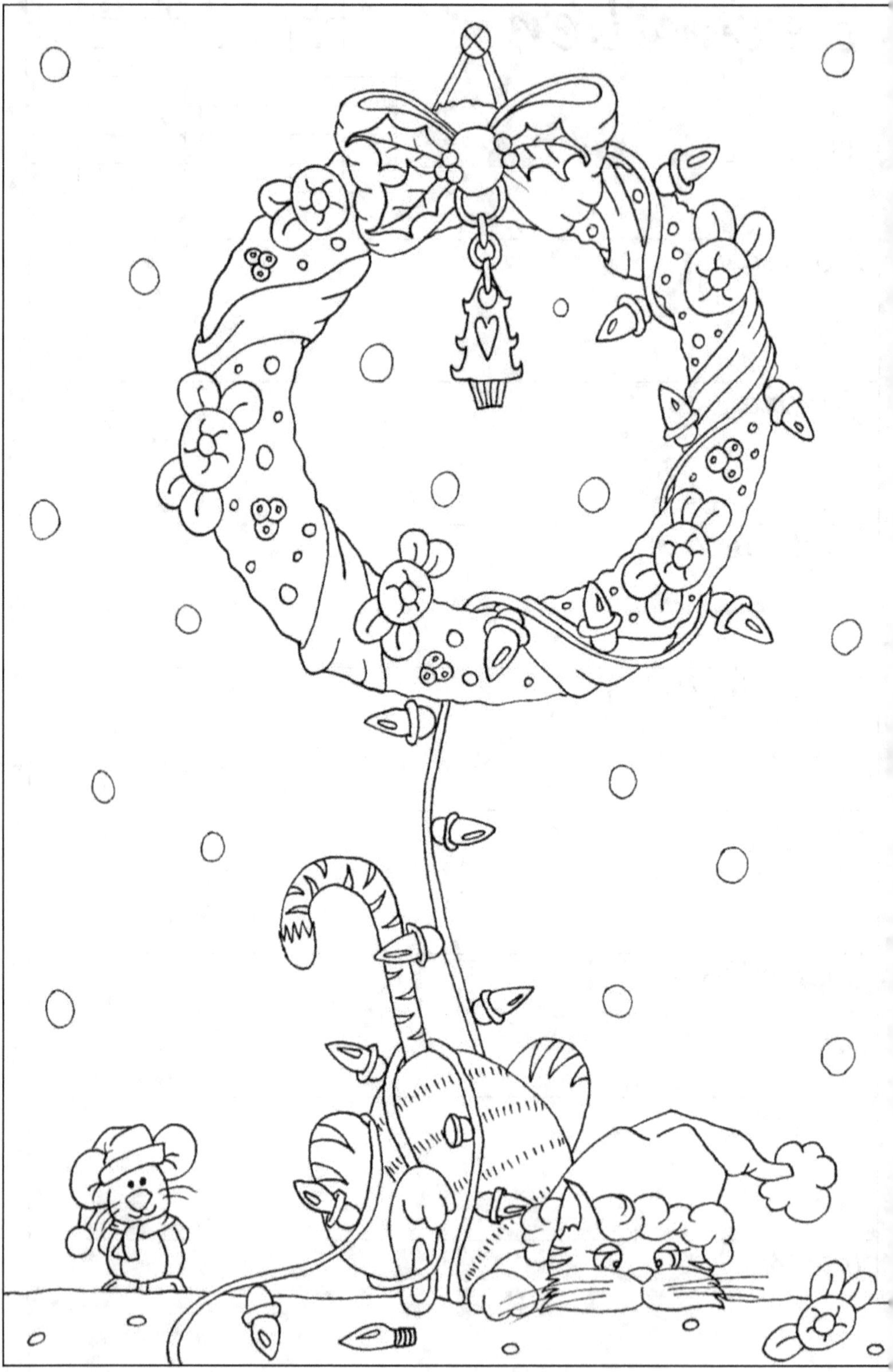

December

WEEK _____

M	T	W	T	F	S	S

Monday
Tuesday
Wednesday
Thursday
Friday
Saturday
Sunday
Notes

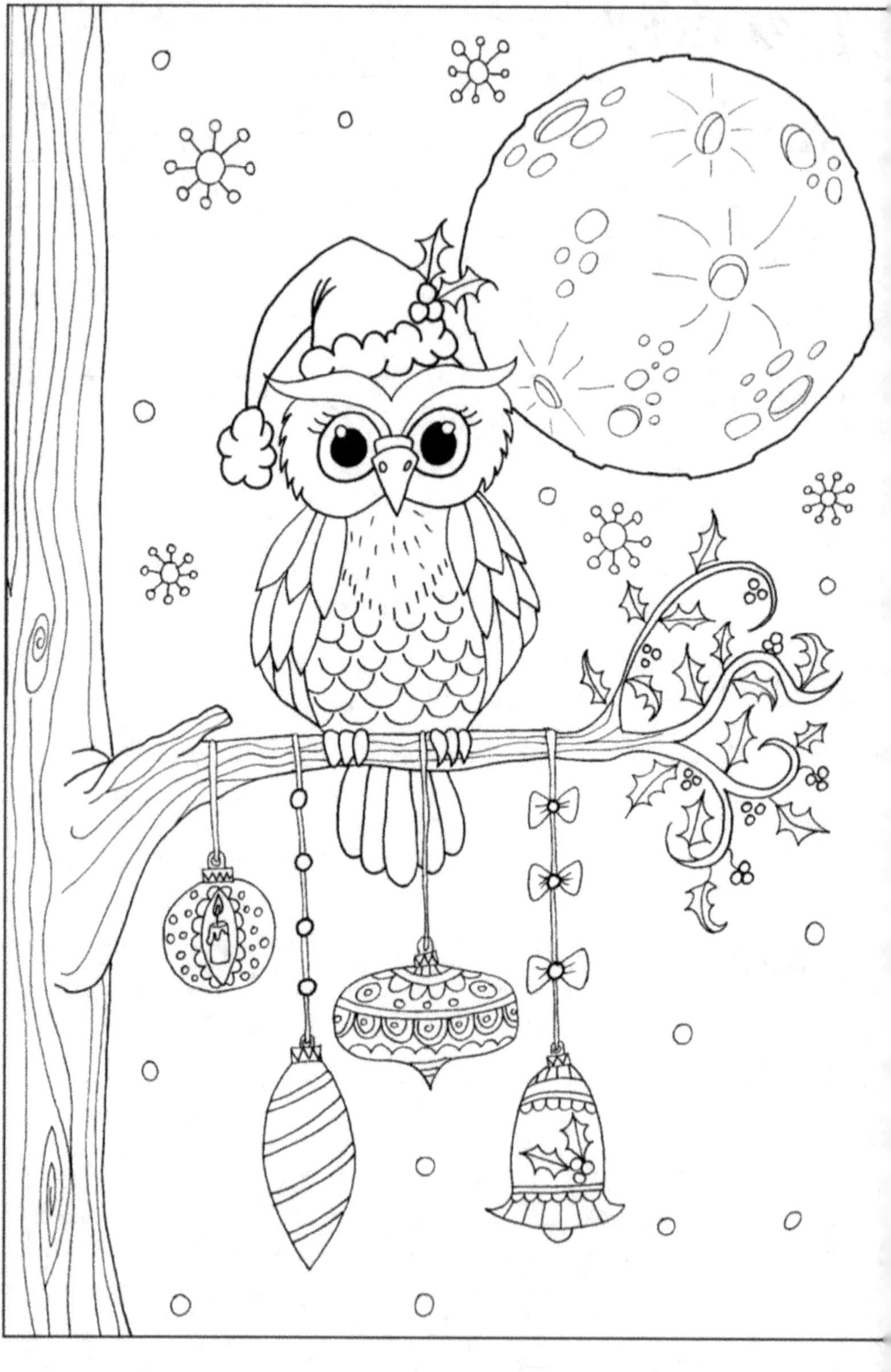

December

WEEK _____

M	T	W	T	F	S	S

Monday

Tuesday

Wednesday

Thursday

Friday

Saturday

Sunday

Notes

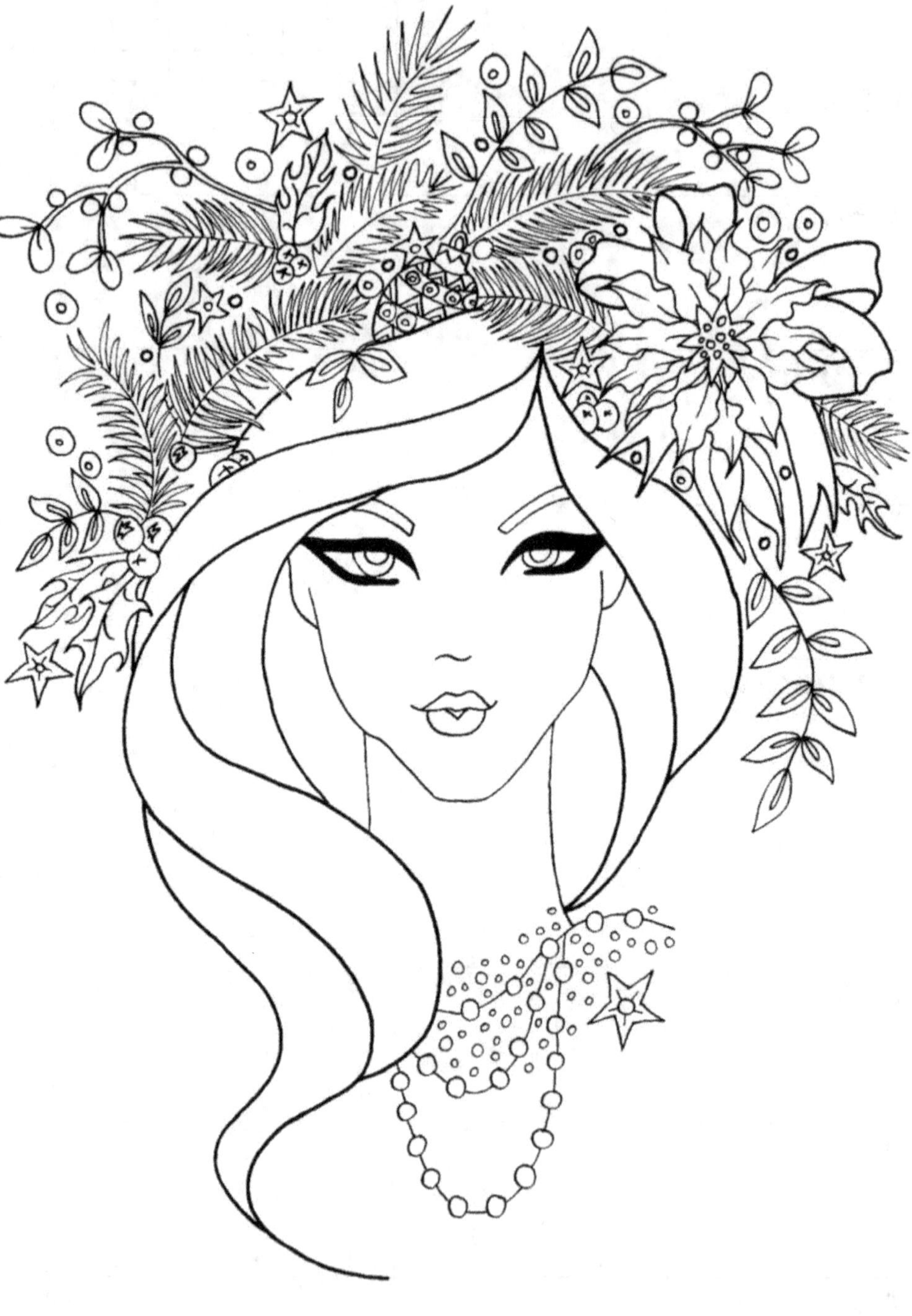

December

WEEK _____

M	T	W	T	F	S	S

Monday

Tuesday

Wednesday

Thursday

Friday

Saturday

Sunday

Notes

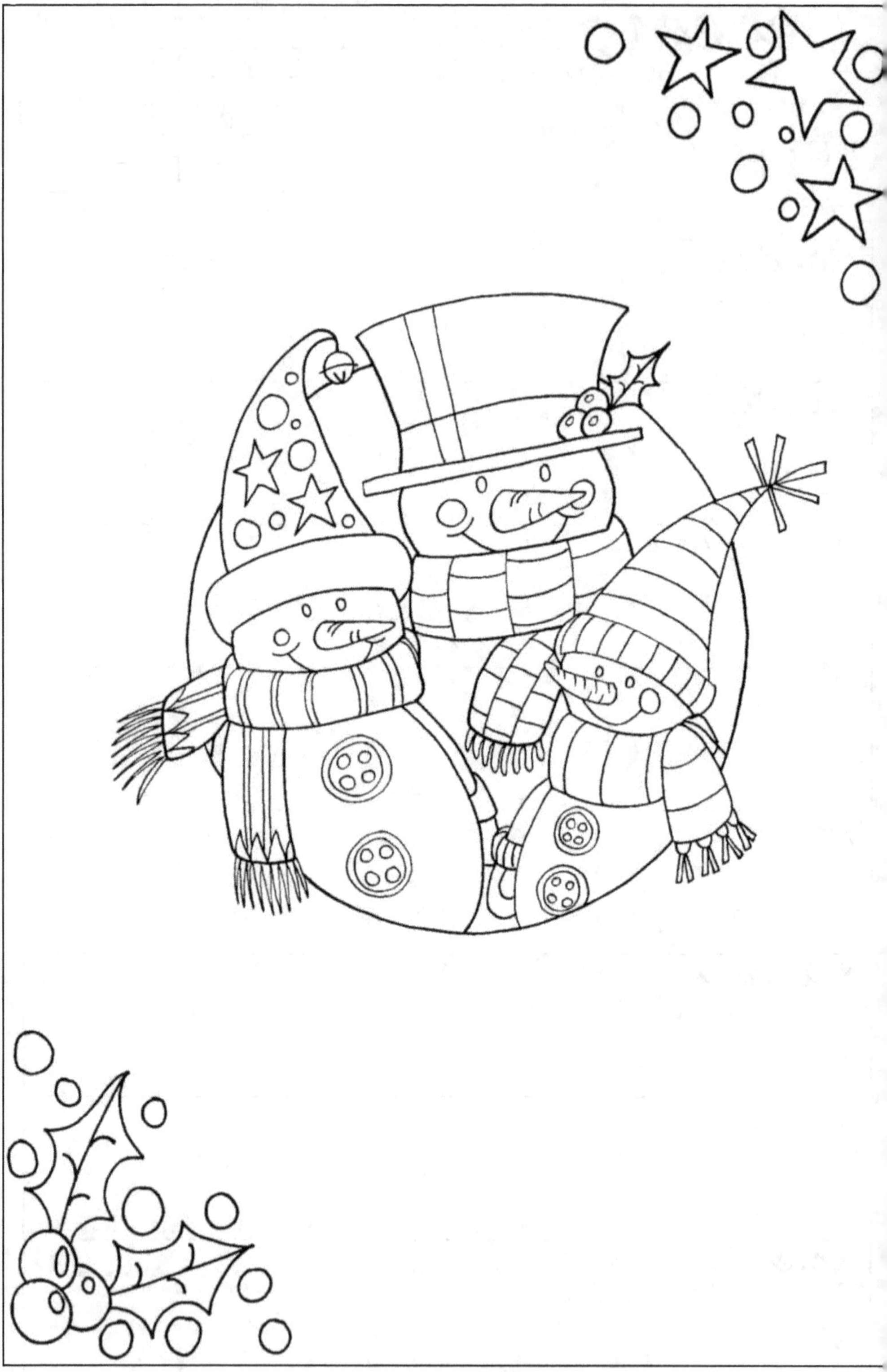

December

WEEK _____

M	T	W	T	F	S	S

Monday
Tuesday
Wednesday
Thursday
Friday
Saturday
Sunday
Notes

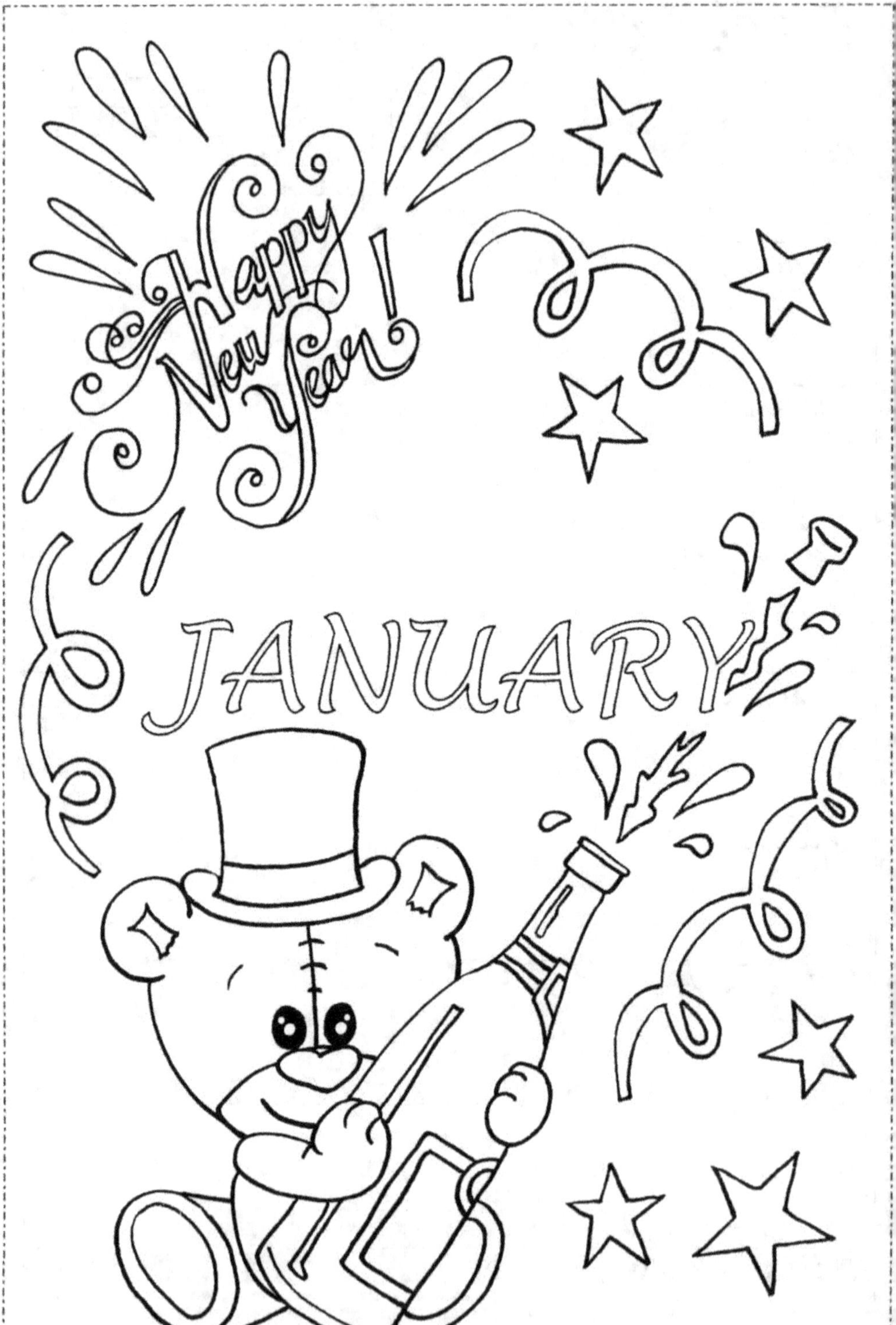
Happy New Year!
JANUARY

Month at a glance …

January

M	T	W	T	F	S	S

January To Do:

- ○ ________________________________
- ○ ________________________________
- ○ ________________________________
- ○ ________________________________
- ○ ________________________________
- ○ ________________________________
- ○ ________________________________
- ○ ________________________________
- ○ ________________________________

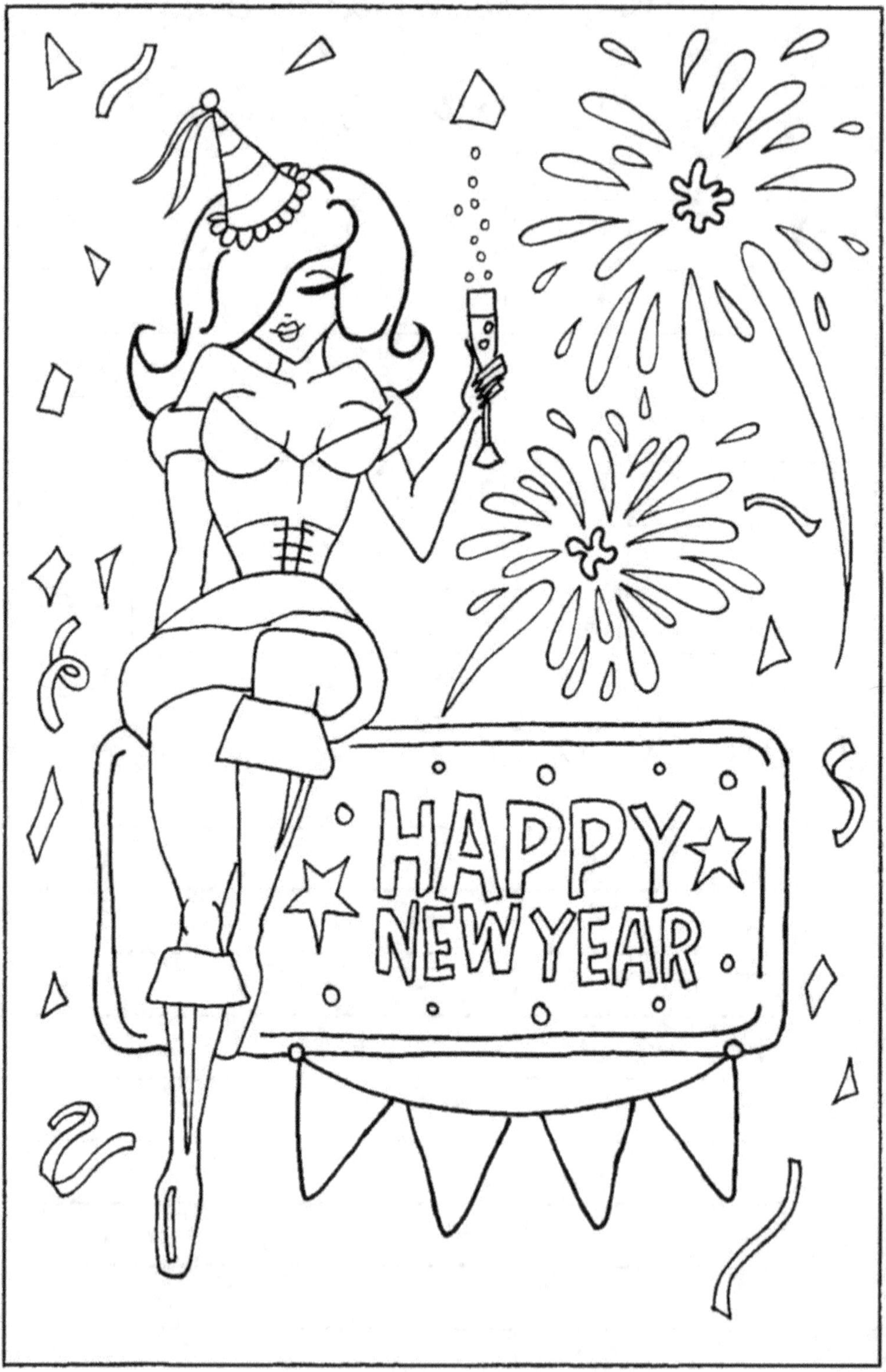
HAPPY
NEW YEAR

January

WEEK _____

M	T	W	T	F	S	S

Monday
Tuesday
Wednesday
Thursday
Friday
Saturday
Sunday
Notes

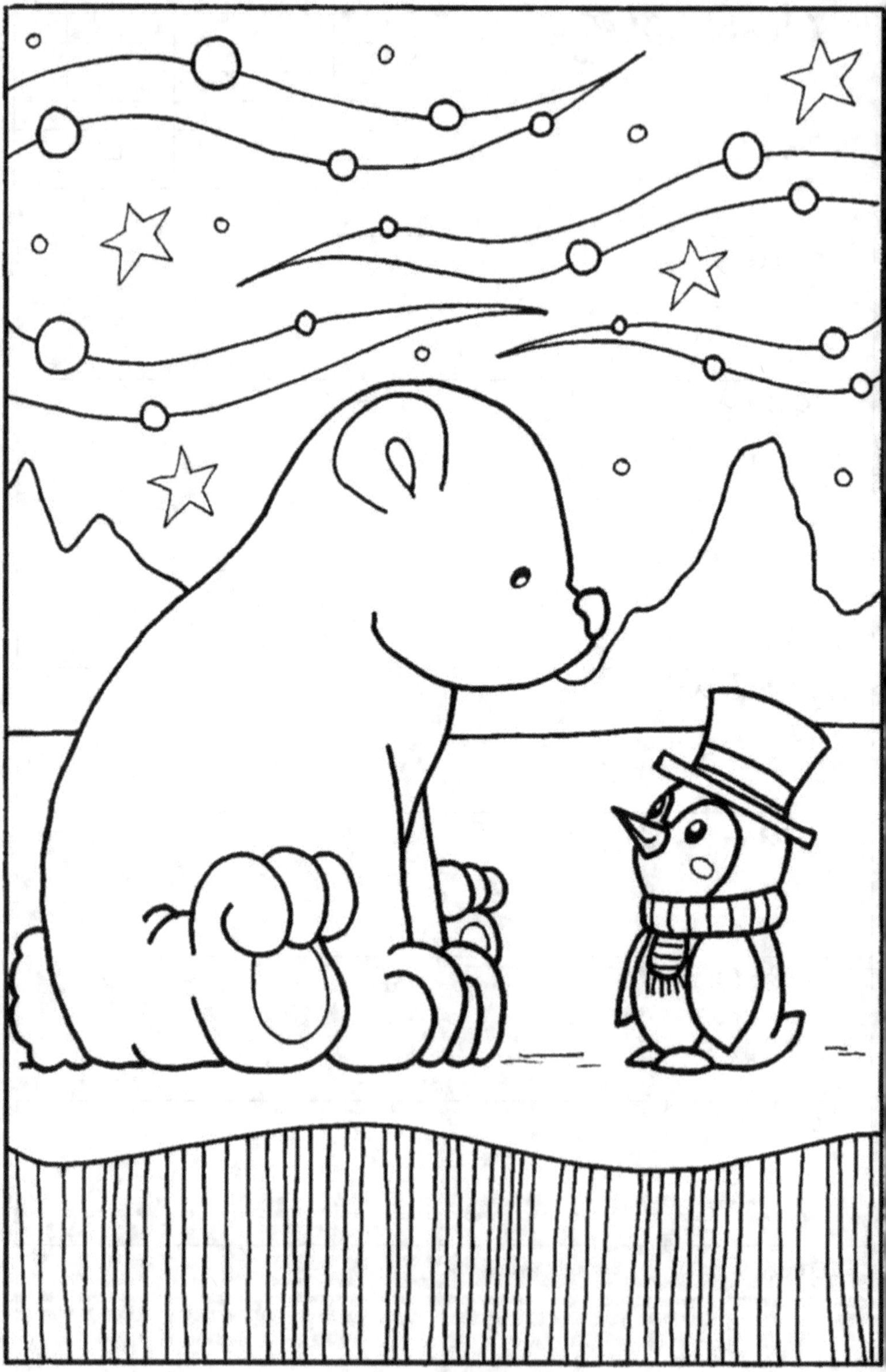

January

M	T	W	T	F	S	S

WEEK _____

Monday
Tuesday
Wednesday
Thursday
Friday
Saturday
Sunday
Notes

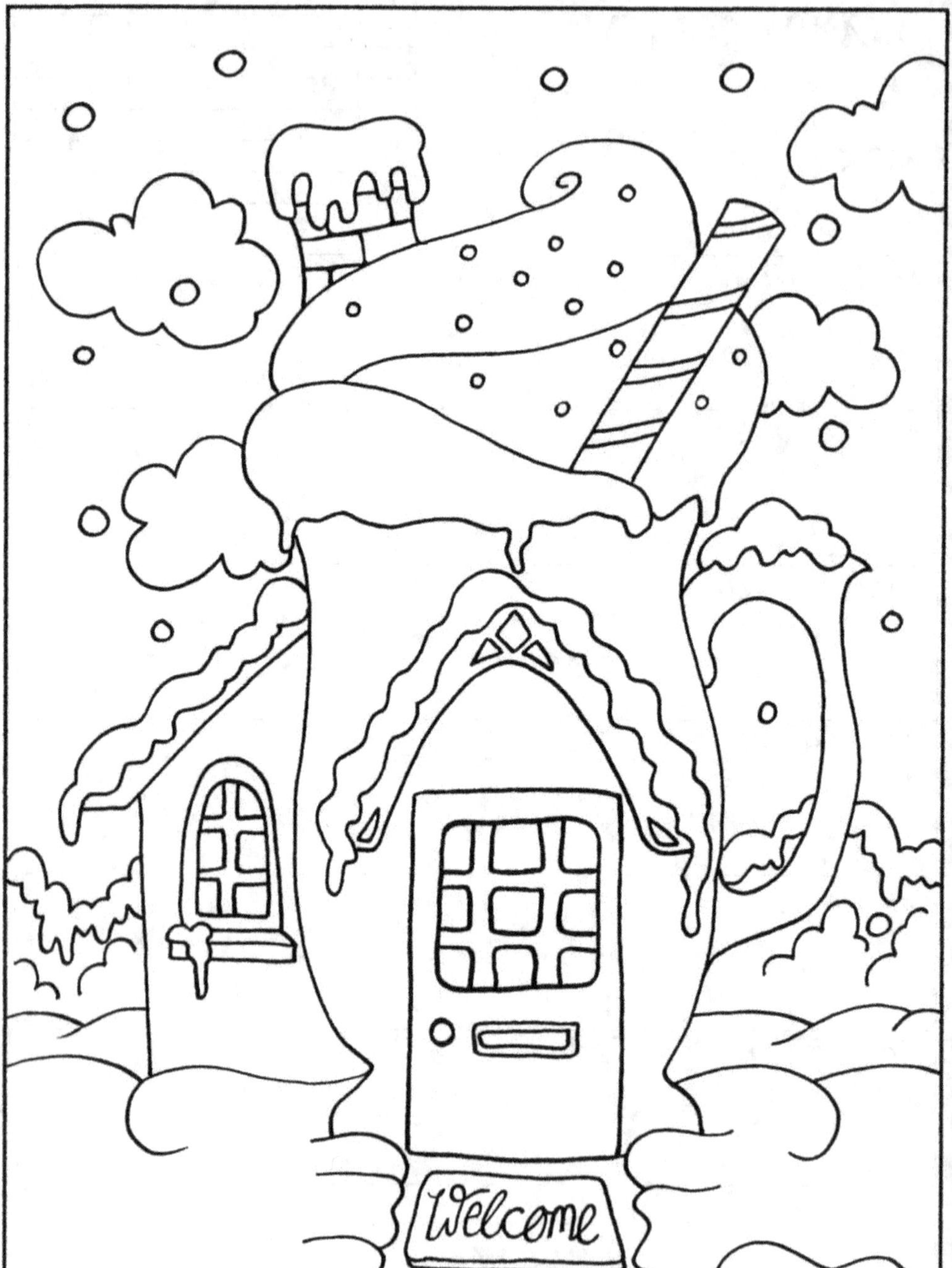
Welcome

January

WEEK _____

M	T	W	T	F	S	S

Monday

Tuesday

Wednesday

Thursday

Friday

Saturday

Sunday

Notes

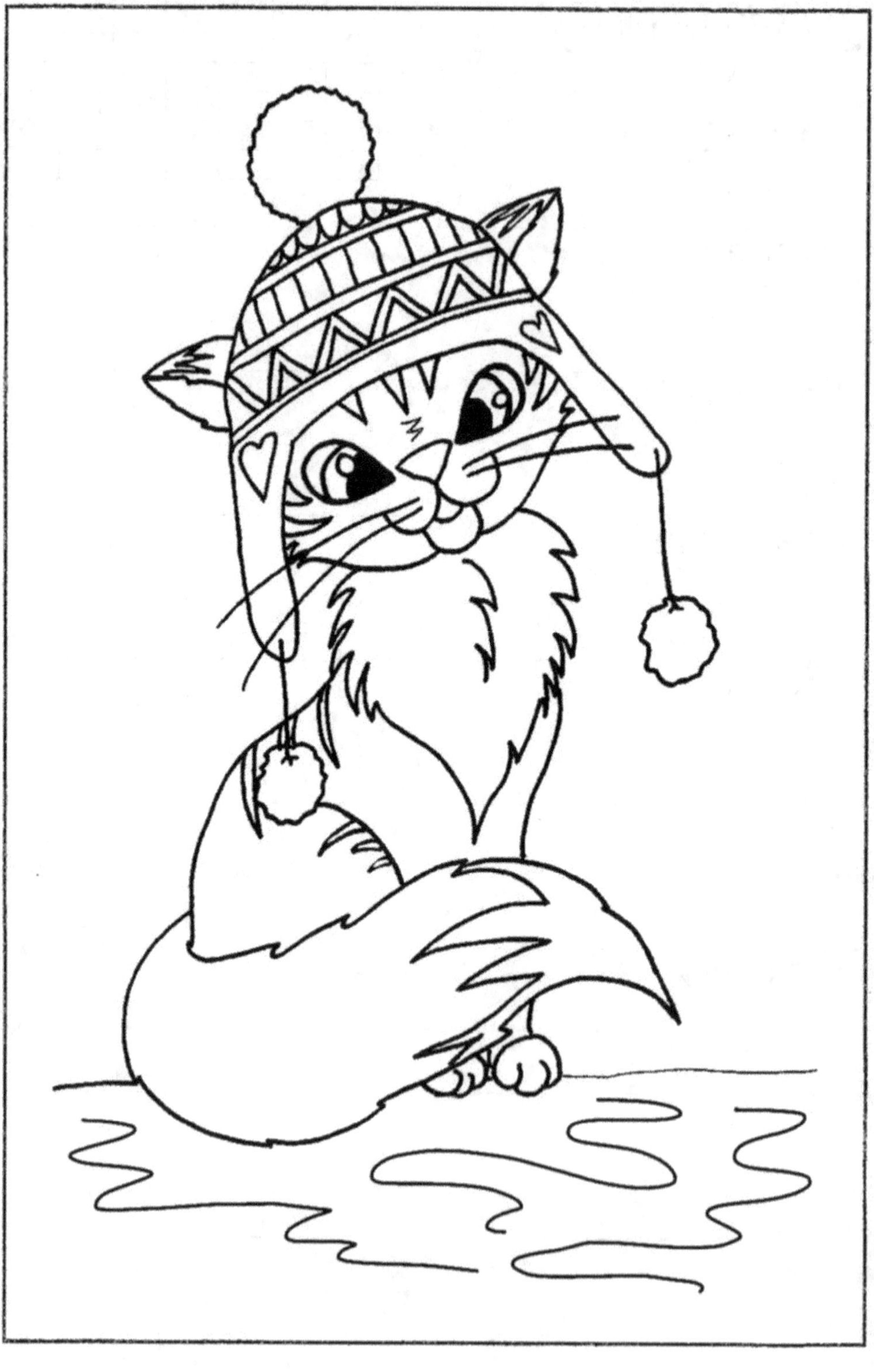

January

WEEK _____

M	T	W	T	F	S	S

Monday

Tuesday

Wednesday

Thursday

Friday

Saturday

Sunday

Notes

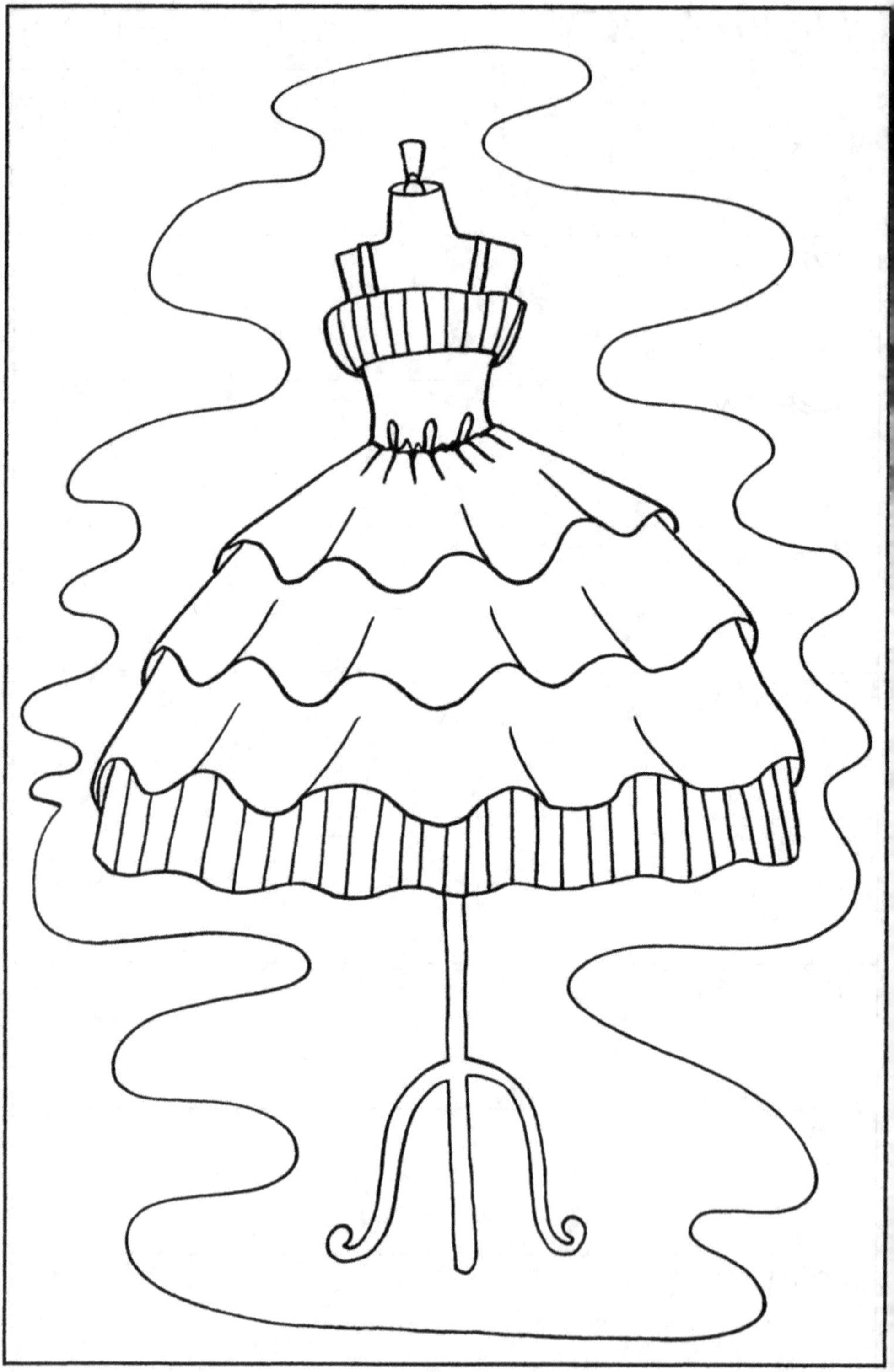

January

WEEK _____

M	T	W	T	F	S	S

Monday
Tuesday
Wednesday
Thursday
Friday
Saturday
Sunday
Notes

www.ingramcontent.com/pod-product-compliance
Lightning Source LLC
Chambersburg PA
CBHW051311220526
45468CB00004B/1296
* 9 7 8 1 9 7 4 5 0 2 2 8 8 *